"In this collection of true stories, the An████ ⚘ █████████████
serve as conduits for messages of spiritual love and help in times of
despair, loss, and confusion. Meditations following each story guide
those in need of some soul work, making the book even better....
Pick up several copies as gifts for all the animal lovers on your list.
Yes, it really is that good!"

— *Best Friends* magazine

"Aims straight for the heart...The experiences shared in the book
offer evidence that animals are much more than mere companions
and servants."

— *Today's Woman*

"This well-written book will appeal to anyone who has ever looked
into an animal's eyes and felt as if an angel was looking back."

— *New Age Retailer*

"Stories are moving and well told....Many of the sketches are tributes
to animals — dogs, cats, horses, dolphins, snakes, squirrels, you
name it — that rescued or comforted or inspired their humans. ...
All the stories are purpose driven, either including a lesson or followed by personal questions for reflection."

— *Publishers Weekly*

"Illustrates how traditional cultures have viewed animals as messengers and mediators of the Divine, which is a lesson we need to re-
learn. The book is a bold reminder that consciousness takes many
forms and is not restricted to humans."

— *Long Island Press*

"It is not a coincidence that *God* spelled backwards is *dog* and that a lifeline is three-quarters feline. Read this wonderful book and learn to live a complete life."

— Bernie Siegel, MD, author of *Love, Medicine & Miracles*
and *365 Prescriptions for the Soul*

"*Angel Animals Book of Inspiration* opens our eyes to the possibilities available to every one of us at any moment. Allen and Linda Anderson understand the power of our animal connection and that animals give us unconditional love, truth, and spiritual fulfillment. Savor each story, rich in spirit, and learn from our blessed creatures how precious life really is."

— Jackie Waldman, author of *The Courage to Give*
and *Teens with the Courage to Give*

"There is goodness in every page, in every word of this incredible book. It clearly and honorably speaks the truth that the animals, spiritual beings in their own right, offer us the Divine in tangible form. What a gift and invaluable tool Allen and Linda Anderson have given us all."

— Rita M. Reynolds, author of *Blessing the Bridge:
What Animals Teach Us about Death, Dying, and Beyond*

"*Angel Animals Book of Inspiration* awakens us to the truly divine essence of our animal companions and their remarkable devotion to humanity. This is a book to savor and share!"

— Judith Guggenheim, after-death communication researcher
and coauthor of *Hello from Heaven!*

"Every story in this fabulous book is a jewel that will open your heart to love, healing, and faith in all things good. Our relationship with animals is precious, one of God's greatest gifts. Linda and Allen Anderson honor this gift in a most beautiful way."

— Rosemary Ellen Guiley, PhD,
author of *Breakthrough Intuition: How to Achieve a Life of Abundance by Listening to the Voice Within*

"The Andersons celebrate our relationship with animals and explain why we often feel spiritually connected with them. This book is an inspiring compilation of stories, pictures, and anecdotes that warm the heart and feed the soul."

— Mary Hessler Key, PhD,
author of *What Animals Teach Us* and *The Entrepreneurial Cat*

ANGEL ANIMALS
book of inspiration

ANGEL ANIMALS
book of inspiration

Divine Messengers of
Wisdom and Compassion

ALLEN AND LINDA ANDERSON

NEW WORLD LIBRARY
NOVATO, CALIFORNIA

New World Library
14 Pamaron Way
Novato, California 94949

Copyright © 2003 by Allen and Linda Anderson
Originally published as *God's Messengers* in 2003.

Permissions acknowledgments appear on page 218.

Text design and typography by Tona Pearce Myers

Library of Congress Cataloging-in-Publication Data
God's messengers.
Angel animals book of inspiration : divine messengers of wisdom and compassion / Allen and Linda Anderson ; foreword by Allen M. Schoen.
    p.   cm.
Originally published: God's messengers. Novato, Calif. : New World Library, c2003.
Includes bibliographical references (p. 215).
ISBN 978-1-57731-666-4 (pbk. : alk. paper)
1. Animals—Religious aspects. 2. Spiritual life. I. Anderson, Allen, 1954– II. Anderson, Linda C., 1946– III. Title.
BL439.G63 2009
202'.12—dc22   2009009071

First publication as *Angel Animals Book of Inspiration*, May 2009
ISBN 978-1-57731-666-4
Printed in Canada on 100% postconsumer-waste recycled paper

 New World Library is a proud member of the Green Press Initiative.

10   9   8   7   6   5   4   3   2   1

Contents

Part One: Love

Chapter One: How Do Animals Remind Us of the Divine?   3

Chapter Two: Hearing the Whispers of Love   19

Chapter Three: Choosing to Be Together   37

Chapter Four: Angel Animals Heal Hurting Hearts, Bodies, and Minds 55

Part Two: Wisdom
Chapter Five: Are Prayers Answered? 75

Chapter Six: Why Do Bad Things Happen? 89

Chapter Seven: Are We Mirrors for Each Other? 107

Part Three: Courage

Chapter Eight: Angel Animal Heroes   125

Chapter Nine: Do Animals Help Us Have Strength to Survive Troubled Times?   139

Part Four: Comfort

Chapter Ten: Do Dreams of Animals Contain Spiritual Messages?   157

Chapter Eleven: Do Animals Go Peacefully into the Light?   175

Chapter Twelve: Reuniting with Loved Ones   195

Foreword

*A*ngel Animals Book of Inspiration offers a profound exploration of questions that have been pondered by the greatest philosophers, sages, and mystics of all time. Yet the questions in this book are asked and answered from a unique perspective, through the eyes of our animal friends and the deep connection we share with them.

When Allen and Linda Anderson asked me to write a foreword for this book, I was touched and honored based on my appreciation of their previous endeavors to help animals. However, I'll admit I was surprised when I saw the table of contents; I wondered if this would affect my credibility as a veterinarian, professor, and author. Questions such as "Have we gone too far?" and "Is this for real?" ran through my left brain. After I read the introduction and other chapters, my apprehension was quelled by the wonderful balance of sincerity and scientific evidence that the Andersons have smoothly woven into the book.

As a child, I never questioned whether there was a God or whether all animals were part of a bigger picture — an interconnected web of life. I never questioned my connection with animals. There was always an inner knowing of a very deep spiritual connection with all beings. Certainly some of that intuitive knowledge was squelched as I went through veterinary medical school and was trained to believe that the only reality was based on double-blind, placebo-controlled studies. But through my part golden retriever, part canine Florence Nightingale dog, Megan, my heart was reopened. I realized that, although Western medicine offered many beneficial therapies, there was much more to healing than medications and surgery — and that the greatest healer of all is the interconnectedness and unconditional love of all beings.

My journey home to my heartspace was guided by my connection with and love of all animals. Through this connection, I was led back to my deep faith in God and my love and compassion for all beings. Love, compassion, and a belief in God are not proven philosophically, but they can be lived daily in each and every moment as we walk on this earth with our kindred spirits. Allen and Linda have taken the concepts that I share in my books to a whole new level, asking the most profound questions and finding the most wonderful, joyous answers through our animal friends. I am grateful that they have the courage to explore and share the deepest levels of our kindred connections.

I love this book. Read it and open your heart, and transform into the loving beings that we all are!

Blessings to you all.

A kindred spirit,

— Allen M. Schoen, DVM, MS, author of *Kindred Spirits: How the Remarkable Bond between Humans and Animals Can Change the Way We Live* and *Love, Miracles, and Animal Healing*
www.drschoen.com

Golden Connections

Animals and people connect with the same golden threads that weave through all creation. Animal messengers deliver truths and answers about life by touching people's hearts as nothing else can. Animals' instinctive spirituality enables them to interact with their Creator and with creation in ways that can truly be called miraculous. Animals have a talent for bypassing the mind and going straight to the heart.

We are constantly learning our own spiritual lessons with the help of our animal family. That family consists of Leaf, a cute cocker spaniel; Speedy, a shy multicolored tabby cat; Cuddles, a gracious black-and-white kitty; and Sunshine, a cockatiel curmudgeon. These animal companions provide us with insights, unconditional love, and many good laughs.

For over twenty years, as members of the clergy and inspirational authors and speakers, we've focused our attention on discovering and sharing answers to life's most profound mysteries. One thing we've observed is that the animal kingdom serves as a spiritual support system. From around the globe we've collected extraordinary stories about a variety of animals helping people remember that they are never abandoned or alone. The experiences you will read about transcend random acts and synchronicity to show life's precision, wisdom, and beauty.

These stories demonstrate that furry, fuzzy, flowing, and flying creatures have an uncanny ability to serve as a custom-made delivery service for divine love. Some stories are as cheerful as the antics of an animal who helps restore a person's sense of humor. Others are remarkable accounts of visions, miraculous interventions, soul-to-soul communication, or after-death encounters involving animals.

Leaf Anderson

Sprinkled throughout are meditations and exercises you can use for reflection.

The fact is, people are having profound spiritual experiences with animals. The Divine is working through animals as vehicles to bring more love, wisdom, courage, and comfort into the world. Animals are good for human health — physically, mentally, and emotionally. The stories in this book demonstrate that animals are also good for people's spiritual health.

After our book *Angel Animals: Divine Messengers of Miracles* was published, we realized we had tapped into a universal vein of spiritual wealth that has been largely unexplored. We received encouraging letters from well-known animal lovers, including the late Ann Landers, nationally syndicated columnist; Dr. Jane Goodall, noted author and scientist; Tippi Hedren, actress and animal activist; and Valerie Harper, actress. America's most beloved weatherman,

Willard Scott, held *Angel Animals* up to the camera and told viewers of NBC's *Today* show to buy it as "a wonderful Christmas gift." ABC's Peter Jennings featured our book on the nightly news broadcast when he reported findings of a July 2001 ABC News/Beliefnet.com poll; it revealed that 47 percent of people who live with animal companions believe that the souls of pets go to heaven when they die.

Speedy Anderson

Before we go further, we need to explain how we're defining the word *soul*. By *soul* we mean the true and eternal self that never dies. We're differentiating the soul from the physical body, emotions, culture, consciousness, gender, species, or personality. The soul animates the physical body, infusing it with personality, feelings, thoughts, and conscious awareness. At death the soul leaves the body, but it survives in another realm. During life, the soul inspires spiritual impulses such as unconditional love, creativity, imagination, intuition, and free will. As you'll soon see through the stories we're sharing, animals appear to have soul-qualities in abundance.

In this book we refer to God, but you can substitute whatever term you use for Life, the Universe, the Divine, the Goddess, the Sacred, Great Spirit, or a Higher Power. We also don't describe God as male or female or father or mother, although some of the story contributors do.

Our hope is that this book will go beyond individual definitions of who or what God is. Animals don't debate whose God is bigger or better. As vehicles for the Divine, they simply bring comfort by reminding people that goodness, kindness, and love still exist where hatred and loss have left their marks.

We hope the stories we've included will invite you to draw your own conclusions about animals instead of waiting for others to prove or disprove the obvious or the inexplicable. As Kristin von Kreisler writes in her wonderful book *Beauty in the Beasts,* "Scientific experiments are rarely set up to see positive animal behavior." She adds that when she consulted the database at Stanford University, there were

Cuddles Anderson

1,130 studies of animal fear cited and only one about animal courage. "To say the least," she says, "research topics seem to indicate a bias against animals being shown in a positive light."[1]

Yet animals, like humans, run the gamut of spiritual consciousness. Animals are also learning and growing spiritually. This is why it's so beneficial, when pondering questions about God or life, to observe how animals manifest spiritual principles. Animals and humans are cut from the same spiritual cloth by the same divine hand and sustained by the same love.

Many people, including respected members of the scientific community, acknowledge that animals and humans are more alike than we realize. Studies have shown that baboons, chimpanzees, and apes are similar to humans in their mental, cultural, and language abilities.[2]

Animals and humans are also similar in their emotional makeup. Thousands of anecdotes show what anyone who has shared a home with a pet knows: animals display a variety of emotions, including joy, fear, anger, pain, love, grief, and despair. Jane Goodall is quoted as saying that "scientists who use animals to study the human brain, then deny that animals have feelings, are illogical."[3] We agree with Dr. Michael Fox, who decries the "mechanomorphizing" of animals, in which they are viewed as unfeeling machines.[4]

Sunshine Anderson

It is our belief that animals and humans are in partnership on the planet, learning and growing together. If we have social, language, cultural, psychological, and emotional characteristics in common, is the next step a study of our shared spiritual evolution? Could we learn more about the Divine and our own spiritual nature by observing animals?

Human beings look beyond the clouds to the stars and distant planets for answers to questions about life. Yet at our feet, in the branches of our trees, in our rivers and oceans, on our laps, and at our back doors, the eyes of kindred spirits watch and wait for us to recognize the wisdom and compassion of animals.

PART ONE

LOVE

Apprehend God in all things,
For God is in all things.
Every single creature is full of God
And is a book about God.
Every creature is a word of God.

— Meister Eckhart

CHAPTER ONE

How Do Animals Remind Us of the Divine?

According to the Kabbalah, at some point in the beginning of things, the Holy was broken up into countless sparks, which were scattered throughout the universe. There is a god-spark in everyone and everything, a sort of diaspora of goodness. God's imminent presence among us is encountered daily in the most simple, humble, and ordinary ways.

— Rachel Naomi Remen, MD

Is there a God? Wow! What a question! Philosophers, scientists, and stargazers throughout history have asked it. Most people say they believe there is a God. But when life throws an almighty curveball, doubts arise. We ask: If God exists, where was he/she/it when I needed help? In other words, sometimes we need a little tangible support for our belief.

Animals seem to offer us comfort by bringing proof of God's existence. Many people, at the time of their greatest suffering or despair, have experienced the presence of the Divine with the help of animals in their homes or in nature.

The following stories of animals, living in the wild or as companions in homes, remind us that, yes, we are supported in whatever ways are best for our spiritual growth and renewal. Perhaps you will be reminded of times when animals revealed the Divine to you.

The Dog Who Discovered God

Mary Elizabeth Martucci
South Bend, Indiana

*M*ary had a little lamb, but I had my dog, Skippy. Mary's lamb followed her to school each day, but my dog followed me to church each Sunday. We lived a block from the church and often played in the churchyard after school. Skippy knew the territory well, and everyone in the neighborhood, including the priests, knew Skippy.

On Sunday mornings, when Skippy walked with me, he waited at the church's side door. I entered that way, always turning to tell Skippy to sit. I was small, and the door was heavy and hard to open and close. Occasionally it didn't shut tightly. One day, I pulled the door closed and took my usual seat in the pew just opposite the side door, several rows from the main altar.

Mary Elizabeth's Skippy

After a few moments, the sound of shuffling feet and muffled voices from surrounding pews interrupted the quiet. Imagine my reaction when I turned toward the sounds and saw Skippy attempting to squeeze his rather large body through the narrow door opening. He glanced at me as if to say, "Okay?" I felt faint, but managed to mouth a strong, "No!"

Skippy ignored me. He waited a second and then slowly, almost on tiptoe, walked toward the altar. Aghast, I froze in my seat. Skippy crossed in front of the altar, climbed the two steps to the left of the altar table, and turned to face the congregation. With the air of a humble fellow worshiper, Skippy lowered himself onto the carpet.

In those days, the church's altar table faced away from the congregation, and the priest's back was toward the people. How clever, I thought, that Skippy had chosen to place himself out of the servers' path.

Simultaneously with Skippy's arrival, the servers marched out of the sacristy followed by the priest, Father John. A hushed congregation collectively held its breath. I was about to burst. I didn't know what to do. Father John approached the altar. First he caught the eyes of the servers, who were looking at him anxiously. Then he followed their gaze to the left. Skippy lifted his head to meet Father John's eyes as if in greeting. Then my dog calmly lay back down.

Father John proceeded to conduct the Mass without incident. At Holy Communion time, I feared what Skippy would do when he saw me approach the altar rail. I had nothing to be concerned about, though. Skippy watched me come and go without twitching a muscle. He also seemed to sense when the Mass was about to end, because he raised his head and glanced over at Father John, seeming to wait for the final blessing. When the priest and servers withdrew, Skippy walked down the steps and back out the side door.

I managed to get to the door quickly and push Skippy out of the church before the priest or parishioners could get their hands on us.

I knew my next big problem in life would be to explain all this to Mama.

Surprisingly, neither Father John, the members of the congregation, nor my mother reprimanded Skippy or me. I was only reminded to close the door more carefully. Everyone commended Skippy for his exemplary behavior during Mass.

The following Sunday, Skippy and I took off again for church. I entered the side door as usual, and this time I made sure I pulled it tightly closed. After Father John started Mass, I caught a glimpse of Skippy walking toward the altar. I couldn't believe it! Apparently someone had entered the church after me and allowed enough space for Skippy to get in again.

This time, I was certain Father John would oust the dog. I could feel myself growing red-faced with embarrassment as Skippy climbed up one step, then two, and nestled down for Mass. Father John glanced over at him, turned back to the altar, and continued with the service. Was that a smile I saw on the priest's face?

After Mass, Skippy respectfully waited until everyone had left the church. Since this was his second appearance, Skippy now became the talk of the congregation. People stopped to pet him and say what a good dog he had been. They shared their amazement over how the dog seemed to know where to lie and the respect he showed for Father John and the ceremony. Some suggested that Skippy understood what Mass was all about. Most of the people in the parish found Skippy's behavior amusing and inoffensive. Some even thought Skippy had a right to be allowed to attend church on Sunday.

Accepted by the parish, Skippy was welcome at Sunday services from that day on. The high point of the Mass was when the priest raised the chalice and host. Everyone is supposed to be attentive at that time. Many were not, until they started watching Skippy carefully observing the priest's movements at the most sacred moment of the service. I noticed that attendees started to follow Skippy's example by looking up at the chalice when they were supposed to. I think he made everyone more reverent, alert to their reasons for attending weekly Mass, and mindful and respectful of each other. After those first Sundays, someone began to prop open the side door with a wooden block. Skippy no longer had to struggle to squeeze through the opening. For as long as he wanted, God's house was open to him.

Skippy reminded all of us that animals have always served the saints in many ways, most notably Saint Francis of Assisi and Saint Martin de Porres, and have been loved and protected by them in return. When I was eight years old, my dog, Skippy, took the saints up on the promise that even an animal could honor his Creator in church on Sundays.

Meditation

Has an animal ever helped you realize your reverence for the sacredness of creation?

Q: Is There a God? A: Meow!

Mary Ellen "Angel Scribe"
Cottage Grove, Oregon

At twenty-five years old, I began exploring spirituality. I knew there was a God, but I couldn't see or feel God. You might call me a believing skeptic.

Around that time, my husband, Howard, and I took our first vacation together. We rented a motor home and brought along our shaded-silver Persian cats, Channel and Camelot. We left Vancouver Island, Canada, and headed to Lake Chelan in Washington State. At the campsite, we put the cats on their harness-leashes. A short time later, we noticed that Camelot had wiggled free of his harness and was gone.

Of all the animal companions I've loved, this shy, gentle creature most relied on me and trusted that I'd protect him. I had adopted Camelot from someone who raised him in a cage, so the cat had not learned how to fend for himself.

We were devastated at the thought of losing Camelot. We walked around the small town of Lake Chelan calling for him and offering his favorite treat as a reward if he'd return, but to no avail. For the next four days and three nights, we wandered the streets all day and into the wee hours of the morning. We left word of our precious Persian's disappearance at the radio station, newspaper, and local schools, soliciting the help of the townsfolk in the search for our missing cat.

As the sun rose on the last morning of our vacation, we were still walking around the town calling out for Camelot. Since it was 4:00 in the morning and we had to return home, we knew this was our last chance to find him. We had done everything humanly possible, and I recognized that Camelot's fate was out of my hands. At that point, I passed my heart into the hands of God and said, "If you are really out there, if you really exist, please show me where my cat is."

Mary Ellen and Camelot

The most unusual thing happened next. I felt the invisible hands of God — or perhaps the hands of loving angels — on my back. These hands guided me in the opposite direction from where we'd been walking. They then pressured me to turn to the right, walk another block, and walk to the end of the street. I followed their guidance for about a quarter-mile, and then the feeling lifted. I felt confused. "What was that all about?" I wondered.

I called "Camelot" one last time. From under a bush, twenty feet in front of me, a scared, thinner, fluffy, silver Persian cat meowed. Camelot walked out and stood there, waiting for me to pick him up. He blinked his huge, green Disney eyes at me. My heart melted and rejoiced at the same instant.

We carried Camelot back to the trailer and put him in front of the water and food dishes. Channel walked over to him and swatted him on the head with her paw. Her look implied, "You sure caused a lot of trouble."

The story of our missing cat soon spread around the entire town. When we pulled out of the motor home park for the long trip back to Vancouver Island, we told the gatekeeper that we'd found our cat and she burst into tears. She said, "Today is my twenty-first birthday, and finding Camelot safe is the best present anyone could give me." There certainly are kind people all over the world.

Camelot's disappearance for those days helped me discover and understand how the divine power of God works in our lives. The cat's disappearance was mandatory to my spiritual growth. If he had not taken flight, I would never have been desperate enough to pray for the first time in my life — and then have the hands of God/Spirit/Angels lead me to Camelot. For me, this was a miracle — an epiphany.

Is there a God? We must all answer this question in our own way and in our own time. Asking the question seems to be the key. And maybe an animal will help reveal the answer.

Meditation

Could animal messengers be alerting you to divine intervention in your life? Has there been a time when an animal helped you know that the Divine was near?

The Presence of Teddy

Rose-Marie Silkens
Sayward, British Columbia

*T*eddy is a black, tan, and white collie mixed breed. To my eyes, she's a dog of exceptional beauty, and we've been together as best friends and companions for nearly fifteen years. Teddy and I share an understanding based on total mutual commitment to each other. I have never doubted that Teddy would give her life for me without the slightest hesitation. My paltry human love cannot equal her unequivocal devotion. I have always described our relationship by saying, "My dog and I are completely bonded." But I had no idea how true this statement was until I was diagnosed with cancer.

Through the stages of my recovery from three operations, Teddy stayed near me, sleeping beside the bed, watching my every move. She was clearly anxious and upset when I felt uncomfortable or distressed.

Rose-Marie's Teddy

Then came chemotherapy. I had been able to cope with many of the difficulties so far — the loss of body parts, the fatigue, the side effects of medication — but the thought of losing my long hair during chemo plunged me into depression. On the good advice of a cancer nurse, I had my hair cut short at the start of treatment. This would forestall the shock of seeing clumps of it falling out.

Over a three-week period, handfuls of hair separated from my itchy scalp. Each loss brought me greater distress. My coping skills quickly eroded. One evening, I sat in my rocking chair, pulling out tufts of hair and sobbing energetically. Teddy lay on the floor beside me and watched intently. Suddenly she began to pull at the fur on her tail. Before I could stop her, she had ripped out a few clumps.

Teddy's action, of course, stopped my tears and self-pity. I went to bed that night marveling at the depth of this dog's compassion.

The next morning, I found Teddy sleeping in a mass of long black hair. She had yanked out almost all the fur from the midsection of her tail, no doubt with considerable pain. Her beautiful black tail and its white plume now looked like a funny little rat's tail with a pale-colored brush on its end. Then Teddy looked up at me with her devoted little face. It was as if she was willing me to feel better. I could almost hear her saying, "If you have to lose your hair, I'm going to lose mine, too."

Teddy and I both appeared a bit strange that summer. In the fall, when her winter coat came in, Teddy's tail quickly began to look better. My hair took a quite a bit longer to return, but I never cried about it again. Sharing my loss with my best friend Teddy took the sadness away.

Meditation

Has an animal climbed on your lap when you were ill or sad and warmed your heart? What messages have animals conveyed with their actions when you most needed comfort?

Send in the Cows

Monica O'Kane
St. Paul, Minnesota

*O*ne afternoon, while visiting a farm and standing in its pasture, I was bursting with anguish over a personal relationship. My head drooped. My shoulders were crushed with a ten-ton block of grief. Tears flooded my face and soaked my shirt. I pleaded silently, "Somebody please be with me!"

Then, through my watery veil, I saw a herd of about fifteen cows and calves coming out of the woods. Feeling cut off from all human support, I welcomed their presence. Slowly but steadily, the whole herd advanced. At first I feared they were going to chase me out of their pasture, but then I realized that they didn't seem menacing. Some cows walked a wide berth around me and came up from behind. Others ambled straight toward me.

I've been in a pasture with cows before, but none had ever approached me. They'd usually wander timidly away unless a farmer with feed was nearby. But these cows completely encircled me. They each stopped when they came within five feet, seeming to sense what would be comfortable for me. I felt no panic. Instead, I found myself being strangely consoled.

To my surprise, a white-faced cow halted directly in front of me. I watched, transfixed, as a tear formed in one of her eyes and spilled down the side of her nose. At first, I wondered if the cow might have an infection, but when I looked into her eyes I saw that they were perfectly healthy. I concluded that this cow could be empathetic — sympathizing with me as I shed my own tears in her pasture.

Gradually my heaving sobs subsided into noisy gulps. Eventually I cried silently. Meanwhile, the cows seemed to form a barrier between the cause of my turmoil and me. I'd fruitlessly hoped that humans would comfort me this way. In answer to my plea, I'd been visited by a herd of cows. After they moved away, I felt a peaceful calm wash over me.

A year later, in the midst of praying, I suddenly remembered the farm animals who had so unexpectedly visited me in the pasture. I realized that God had been answering my prayer. God was saying, "Don't you remember that collective cow hug I sent you a year ago? I directed my creatures to you, but you didn't recognize my touch, my love. Today you do. But then I ministered to you in your isolated agony through the cows."

I felt gratitude for the bovine hug that had relieved my sadness and reassured me that I'm never alone.

Meditation

Has an animal used an unusual way to help you feel less alone or abandoned?

Season's Eternal Song

Aubrey Forbes
Eden Prairie, Minnesota

In spring in the beaks of birds you can find
Wiggling worms, pumpkin seeds, straw for nests,
And sometimes a song of freedom
Sung by a bright red one, carried

In the sounds of all the seasons
Past summer's whistling winds,
Through the dying, bright,
Crackling yellow leaves of fall and

The imperceptible thud of soft, silent, falling snow.
This freedom song, eerie in its cadence,
Incarnates in a cardinal,
Released in its red voice,

Colors the buds green and gold.
White winter melting into green
Gives birth to spring.
In this same beak, music lessons for the young

And during the quiet time when the leaves are still,
Feathers ruffle the moment,
When the spirit of the song
In a silent hush passes on.

Do animals also let us know that love can be unconditional? The next chapter offers some extraordinary glimpses of love touching human hearts with the help of animals.

CHAPTER TWO

Hearing the Whispers of Love

And the little hills rejoice on every side. The pastures are clothed with flocks; the valleys also are covered with grain; they shout for joy, they also sing.

— Psalm 65:12–13 (NKJV)

*Y*ou've heard of watchdogs who let people know when danger is near, but our yellow Labrador retriever, Taylor, used to let us know when love was lurking. Linda began to notice that when Allen was away and called home, Taylor often knew about it in advance. About a second before the telephone rang, Taylor would come to wherever Linda was and perk up her doggie ears. Then she'd give a short "woof" and nod her head toward the telephone. Within a heartbeat, the phone would ring and Allen was on the other end of the line.

At first, we thought this just happened when Allen, Taylor's favorite person in the world, called. But the mystery of Taylor's ability to tune into the love vibration continued to unfold. We started to notice that sometimes when an animal lover was about to call, Taylor also did her routine: ears up, a short bark, and a look with anticipation toward the telephone. If a caller wasn't approaching us with love, Taylor ignored the incoming signal. We finally concluded that Taylor, along with many of the animals you'll read about in this chapter, has a heightened love detector.

We'd probably all like to be able to recognize love when it is on the way or has arrived. But sometimes love can seem distant or nonexistent. If you envision an impersonal deity in a faraway heaven, how would your life change if you knew that God's love is as close as your own breath? Would you recognize grace more easily if the vehicles for miracles sat on your lap or perched on your shoulder? The stories in this chapter demonstrate that divine love is both near and unconditional, allowing for free will and the range of human experience.

These stories may help you remember times when animals delivered spiritual wake-up calls and then quieted your mind so that you could hear the whisper of divine love.

The Man Who Didn't Like Cats

Lynn Harper
Encinitas, California

*W*hen I married Bill, I knew that he barely tolerated children and animals. Cats were especially unthinkable. He changed his mind about children when our daughter, Liberty, came along. Over the years, he learned to live with our two dogs — Golli, a Yorkie, and Charli, a Maltese — as well as two box turtles and a few guppies. When Liberty turned thirteen, a pivotal age when she needed a creature of her own to love, she decided that she wanted a kitten. I tried to convince her that it would be best to get a cat later; I knew that Bill wouldn't be happy about having a feline addition to our family.

One day, Liberty and I went to a plant nursery, where we noticed on the counter a photo of a litter of kittens. Our hearts melted at the sight of a cute pewter-colored kitten with a white mustache and white chest. One of her white paws had a distinctive pewter mark. Liberty and I looked at each other and said, "This cat is meant to be with us."

The lady at the counter said that the litter had recently been born at her home. The kittens would be ready for new homes in a month. We told her which one we wanted, and she wrote "taken" on that kitten's picture.

Now we had to break the news to Bill. We decided to wait until the kitten was ready to come home. When we finally told him, he glared, gritted his teeth, and said, "That cat is never to come into our bedroom."

When we went to get the kitty, the husband of the lady from the nursery almost gave us the wrong one. But before we left, the woman came home and found our kitten buried deep in the couch cushions on the far side of the room, looking like a queen who had to separate herself from the others. We picked up the kitty and immediately felt a heart connection with her. We said, "This is the

Lynn's Sage

kitten who is supposed to come home with us." Since we'd originally gone to the nursery to buy a sage plant and found the kitten's photo there, we named her Sage.

When we arrived home, Bill only said, "It doesn't go into the bedroom."

Wouldn't you know it? Sage liked Bill right away. As the days and weeks passed, Bill started playing with Sage, letting her bat at things he held for her. Bill was always the first to get up in the morning and, to my surprise, he started sharing his breakfast with Sage. Together they ate fruit, cheese, ice cream, and anything else he had on his plate. It wasn't long before Sage was allowed into our bedroom. In the mornings, she began to hop on the nightstand next to Bill, emitting a distinctive sound like Spanish rolling r's to alert him when it was time to begin their morning ritual. I loved seeing Bill look forward to his early-morning playtimes with Sage. He seemed to genuinely enjoy taking care of her. He nicknamed Sage, who now weighed in at eighteen pounds, "Ms. Americat."

Sage had one big problem that should have caused Bill to reconsider his fondness for her: She stopped using her litter box and began urinating on our bed and on the carpet. Each time Sage had an accident, Bill made excuses for her. He bought new mattresses, tore out soiled carpet, and eventually replaced the carpet with slate flooring. Finally he realized that Sage's litter box was too small. He bought the largest litter box he could find, and Sage never again had a problem. But this ordeal revealed the undeniable truth: A pewter-and-white kitten had won the heart of a self-professed cat hater.

The extra dimension that Sage has added to Bill's life is immeasurable. Theirs is a special relationship, and Sage brings him remarkable pleasure. This cat has such a calming effect on Bill that he's become mellower. Sage has brought the quality of unconditional love into Bill's life. She adoringly follows him everywhere.

I always know when Bill is coming home, because Sage apparently senses it in advance. She walks over and sits by the door to the attached garage a few minutes before Bill arrives, when he is a few blocks away. I know from Sage's position that the outside garage door will soon open and Bill will come into the house, where she waits to greet him.

Sage is our wonderful angel animal. We treasure the blessings she's given to our whole family, but especially to Bill.

Meditation

Can you think of a time when an animal's love and compassion has inspired you to respond more lovingly to others? Has an animal showed you that your capacity to love unconditionally is greater than you thought?

A Triple Play of Unconditional Love

Ron Mirolla
Oceanside, California

*W*hen I lost my dog of sixteen years to cancer, I was in great pain. I didn't think I could replace her. Then one day I rode my bike past the Humane Society. I don't know what pulled me in there, but I stopped. I saw a dog named Triple who reminded me of the dog I'd lost, so I approached her cage. She was half German shepherd and half Aussie shepherd, weighing in at about fifty-five pounds. I thought she was beautiful.

When I stopped by her kennel, Triple barked and huddled in the corner. She trembled and urinated. A shelter worker told me that this dog had been beaten every day of her life for over a year. She was, understandably, a very frightened animal.

I left the shelter feeling pain in my heart for this suffering creature. For the next three weeks, I found myself returning to visit her often. Finally, the shelter staff person told me that if I would take a chance, Triple would become the best friend I ever had.

I took that chance, and the shelter woman was so right. Triple not only blossomed into my best friend but also became my teacher. She loved everything — cats, dogs, chipmunks, people. She taught me how to accept and give love.

Two years ago, I moved into a condo complex. Four wild cats inhabited this place. Within a month, Triple had made contact with all four felines. To the amazement of everyone but me, the cats would rub against Triple and purr. After living with her for eleven years, I had come to expect this type of behavior; I knew the effect that her generous heart had on others.

Perhaps the most incredible lesson Triple taught me happened about a year ago. We were walking on the beach when I spotted an old man. He was lying on the rocks, looking dirty and disheveled.

Ron's Triple

Ordinarily, when we went for a walk Triple never left my side. Even when we backpacked in the wilderness, she always stayed with me. But after we'd walked about twenty yards past this old man, Triple turned and ran back to him.

I was so surprised that I couldn't respond until she was already with him. By the time I got to where they were, the man was sitting up with Triple nuzzled against him. He began to pet her, and a smile came to his face.

I ran up and apologized to the man, saying, "I hope my dog didn't startle you."

He slowly looked up at me and said, "This is the first thing that has shown me any love in as long as I can remember."

Tears came to my eyes. I gave the man a ten-dollar bill and bid him a good day. As we left, I looked at Triple and told her that she is my guru, my teacher.

Shortly after this incident, Triple died of cancer. I feel lost without her, and I'll miss her until the day I die.

I buried Triple's ashes at Mammoth Lakes, California, where we had backpacked together. It was a difficult trip — the first time in thirteen years I had been there without her. In my mind's eye, I could see her smile as I hiked the trails we used to walk together. Now when I return to these places, Triple will always be there to watch over me as she did in life — my guardian angel, my gift from God.

God's Love and the Snake

Samuel Dufu
Tema, Ghana, West Africa

$\mathcal{I}$ was born in 1939 and lived in a farming community in what was then called the Gold Coast, now Ghana. When I was three years old, my grandmother carried me on her back everywhere she went. One day, she set me down under an orange tree on her farm. She plucked some oranges, cut them up, and put them in a bowl. I played with the fruit while Grandmother worked thirty feet away, weeding the patches of plantain, cassava, and corn.

As I sucked on the juicy oranges, I threw the peels a few feet from me. My eyes scanned the tufts of nearby vegetation until I noticed something moving in the brush. As if out for a leisurely stroll, a long yellowish snake came toward me and stopped where I'd thrown the peels. I was fascinated by my visitor and tossed more slices to him. The snake returned my friendly gesture by staying around and sucking on the sweet fruit. This interaction went on for about ten minutes before my grandmother overheard me jabbering to my new playmate.

Grandmother approached stealthily. She was astounded to see a deadly snake within biting distance of her precious grandchild, slowly sucking on oranges. With lightning speed, she screamed and whisked me away. My new friend bolted, probably wondering, as I did, what had caused all this commotion.

All the way home, my grandmother's scolding made it clear that snakes are one of our deadliest enemies. Because I had known no natural fear and even made friends with the fruit-loving snake, a rumor started and spread throughout my family that I was endowed with special powers as a snake charmer. A few years later, at school and through the oral tradition of our tribe, I was taught that snakes were dangerous. I then realized the grave danger I'd been in as a toddler and developed a great fear of snakes.

However, because of the spiritual education I've received over the past twenty years, I now understand my childhood experience with the snake more deeply. In short, divine love was at play between two souls — the snake and me. This love left no space for fear. The snake advanced, knowing that I had no intention of harming him but that I only offered love by sharing what I ate. I entertained and encouraged the snake to stay because I had no fear he would bite me. We both enjoyed a friendly moment until my grandmother introduced fear into the harmonious atmosphere. This led to my replacing love with mistrust and hate. My experience with the snake has taught me that, indeed, love conquers all. So it also is with the human family.

Meditation

Do you recall when an animal has been an instrument to help you replace fear with divine love?

The Journey of Joy

J. Blair Taylor
Dexter, Wisconsin

*A*fter reading *Angel Animals: Divine Messengers of Miracles,* I knew I had to find a way to give love to my animal friends. I started on my quest by asking, "What do I have to give?"

Surprisingly enough, I didn't hear a thing from God. While I waited for an answer, I started doing whatever I could think of. I called local animal rescue organizations, offering photography services or anything else they might need. One shelter suggested that I give foster care to a dog, but I preferred not to do this. I already had a dog, a cat, two rabbits, and a husband who was stretched to his limit of appreciation for pets in our home. Every avenue I pursued ended at a brick wall. I began to get discouraged.

"Great! God doesn't want my help," I grumped. "If this is the way it has to be, so be it; I give up. But, God, I will add here that you are turning down the help of someone who really wants to give."

The next day — and I mean the very next day — my neighbor brought me an injured Eastern cottontail rabbit. This baby was the lone survivor of a dog attack. Because I had two domestic rabbits, my neighbor thought I might be able to help.

This little rabbit fit into the palm of my hand. In very poor condition, he had been without sustenance and warmth for twenty-four hours.

I did the only thing I could think of and read a book about helping domestic rabbits in distress. That gave me some ideas, which I applied. Soon the rabbit began to improve.

Then I started having dreams about what I ought to do to help him further. One night, I dreamed that the rabbit was happily splashing around in a shallow container filled with water. So the next morning I gave him a dish of water like the one I'd seen in my dream, and he happily jumped right into it. I had set up his living environment like the ones that satisfy domestic rabbits. But then I dreamed of making this wild rabbit's temporary home more like the one into which he'd be released, with dirt, grass, twigs, and sticks. I learned later that a rabbit's nervous system is delicate, easily thrown off balance. The type of setting I saw in my dream was essential for helping the animal become accustomed to the smells and textures of his future home.

J. Blair's rabbit

It was amazing how much joy and love came from caring for this rabbit. I felt that I had finally found my way to serve. On the day when he was able to go back into the wild, I was thrilled.

Caring for and successfully releasing this rabbit led me to an organization called Friends of Wildlife. I went through their training program, and I am now a licensed wildlife rehabilitator. During the training, I learned how special my first experience with the rabbit had been. There is so much that can easily go wrong. It's important to keep animals' body temperature just right, hydrate them properly, and put them in the correct home environment. If the animals are rehabilitated incorrectly, their lungs can fill with formula and they will be susceptible to pneumonia. If they're not released at the right age, they will kill themselves trying to get free. And it's preferable to rehabilitate the animals in pairs so that they bond with their own species and not with humans. I am so grateful that, against all odds, my dreams helped me give that first rabbit the care he needed.

This year alone, I have cared for eighteen rabbits and six squirrels. The squirrels have deepened my love and appreciation for what I am doing. Each squirrel has a distinct personality and an ability to show gratitude. It is easier for me to bond with squirrels because, depending on their age, they stay with me for about ten weeks through several stages of development. I always miss them when they go. After months of being back out on his own, one squirrel found my second-floor bedroom window. He sometimes visits me by sitting on the window ledge — most often when I've been thinking about him a lot.

The happiness I feel when I'm helping animals get back to their natural habitats is amazing. I have experienced so much love with them. Wildlife rehabilitation isn't something I would have chosen on my own, but through God's grace and love, I have found my own special way of giving. Every day I look for ways to help my animal friends; it is my journey of joy.

Meditation

Are you being shown, perhaps with the help of an animal, how to express your love for life? Are you experiencing the love of the Divine through your own journeys of joy?

Max's Miracle of Love

Meg MacZura-Betts
Granite City, Illinois

For ten years, my dad and mom enjoyed the companionship of my family's black-and-tan cocker spaniel, Max. With his white beard and chest and his big black eyes, he looked like he was wearing a tuxedo and ready for a party. Until my father became ill, my parents babysat Max every day while my husband and I worked.

Eventually, Dad fell into a coma and was hospitalized. One day when the nurses doubted that he would survive the night, they prepared our family for his death. Knowing the special bond between my father and Max, I decided to ask his nurse if I could bring the dog to see him. Much to our surprise, the visit was approved. On the night of my father's expected demise, a hospital security staff member escorted us to the intensive care unit.

When I placed Max next to my father, the dog immediately covered Dad's face and neck with wet kisses. As we all stood and watched this display of love, my father's head suddenly began to move from side to side. Miraculously, a smile appeared on his face. He knew his Max was there and he seemed to be aware of his family, too!

Much to everyone's amazement, Dad's vital signs began to return to normal. He survived that night after Max's visit, and lived to see many more.

Meg's Max

As word spread of this miracle of love between man and animal, Max and Dad became instant celebrities in the hospital. Max was given unlimited visitation rights to see his grandpa, and staff from throughout the hospital visited to witness my father's pet therapy. For the next several months, Max could be found lying across my father's lap.

Even the best medicines and miracles couldn't keep my father alive forever, and we eventually lost him. But the bond between my father and Max lives on. Whenever we visit Dad's grave site, Max sniffs the area and then lies across the grave.

Our family calls Max our hero. We believe this dog is a wonderful example of how a miracle can be created through love.

A Coyote's Message

Kathia Haug Thalmann
Pazzallo, Switzerland

*W*hile I was on holiday in the United States from Switzerland, I participated in a two-week transformational workshop in the California desert with fifteen other people. The workshop activities enabled me to face my childhood fears. At one point, we attendees were on silent retreat in our hotel for three days. This isolation, combined with thinking about my youth, caused me to have insomnia. One night, after finally getting to sleep, I awoke from a dream in which a wild beast was attacking me. I knew this dream was related to the fears I was trying to face, instead of running away from them as I had in the past.

After the dream I couldn't get back to sleep, so at about 4:00 in the morning I went outside to soak in the hot tub in the garden. I was thinking about how, during these three days of silence, I had had many memories of my parents. I remembered that they never made time to spend with me and did not give me any physical warmth. During my early childhood, I did not feel that my mother wanted or loved me.

Before going on this retreat, I had always tried to be strong and brave in my daily life. I did not permit myself to have fears or to be weak. I never asked for love from anyone. But now, sitting in the hot tub, I found myself asking for help. As I soaked in the soothing waters, I started to reflect on a question: What is love? So I asked God, "Please show me what love is."

Then it seemed as if I drifted into another world, where I saw many wild animals living peacefully together. This was a wonderful place, and I didn't want to leave it. But my reverie was interrupted by the sensation of something licking my hand. I turned around and was met by a pair of sparkling eyes looking into mine with such great tenderness that I felt no fear, even though they belonged to a wild coyote!

I have never been afraid of dogs. Quite the opposite; I love them. But coming from Switzerland, I had never seen a wild dog in my entire life, and we don't have coyotes in that part of the world.

When I looked into the coyote's eyes as he licked my hand, my question was answered: This is love. In my dream that night, the wild beast had symbolized my fears. Now I felt that I was being given a chance to choose between living life with fear and living it with love as my constant companion. In that moment with the coyote, I chose love. This experience changed my attitude — and my whole life. I no longer had to push love away from me. It had come to me as an unexpected visitor in the night, and it would stay with me forever.

Meditation

Would you like to try Kathia's question and ask, "What is love?"

CHAPTER THREE

Choosing to Be Together

Having abandoned egotism, strength, arrogance, desire, enmity, property; free from the notion of "mine" and peaceful, he is fit for becoming Brahman.

— The Bhagavad Gita, Dis. XVII: 53

We've always felt that before this lifetime, we must have made a soul agreement with our cat Cuddles, because she came to us exactly when we needed her most. When we began publishing the *Angel Animals Newsletter,* it quickly became successful — probably because it was unique and it filled many people's need to read about spiritual experiences with animals. Much to our surprise, the newsletter attracted the attention of almost every major newspaper and television station in our area. Reporters and photographers started pulling up in vans and parking outside our modest suburban Minneapolis home. Media coverage was both a surreal and fun experience.

Shortly before having our pictures in the paper and being interviewed on radio and television, we began to get those inner nudges from Spirit that say it's the right time to do something. We both felt guided to add a kitten to our family.

We decided to adopt a cat from an animal shelter since these animals desperately need homes. When we opened one of the cages at our local shelter, a tiny black kitten with paws that looked like they'd been dipped in white paint leaped over the others and jumped into our outstretched hands. Her eagerness to be with us gave the impression that she was also choosing us to be her new family. Since she was obviously an affectionate kitty, we decided to name her Cuddles.

Cuddles quickly showed us one of the reasons why she'd adopted us. When the newspaper and television crews started doing stories about us, Cuddles took on the role of the Anderson family's good-will ambassador. She greeted reporters at the door, escorted them into our home, contorted herself for perfect photo ops, interrupted conversations whenever we grappled for the right words, and became indispensable for charming the press. Cuddles was a publicist's dream. It was as if millions of fans were meant to adore her. If she'd signed a photo release, it would have stipulated: To be used for drawing attention to stories that show how adorable animals can be.

Now we invite you to lean back in your easy chair and enjoy the stories of animals whose lives intertwined with others at exactly the right place and time. In some of these stories, it's clear that the pet and the person chose each other. In other cases, animals have shown an unmistakable affinity for someone special. And some stories show animal messengers serving as matchmakers. Each of these stories uniquely answers the question: Do we choose to be together?

Abbie Knew Best

Donna Francis
Savoy, Texas

*F*or over a month, I'd been volunteering at my local SPCA and looking for the perfect dog to bring home. I thought I'd be the one to do the choosing. What I didn't realize was that a certain little dog would also have something to say about the matter. God tried to steer me toward the correct choice, but I wouldn't listen.

The dog I imagined adopting would be pretty, with long flowing hair like a cocker spaniel or a sheltie. Although these physical characteristics were negotiable, I had one steadfast criterion: My new dog had to be a girl.

One day, the ugliest litter of pups I'd ever seen came into the shelter. People called them "spider dogs" because of their long skinny legs. The pups had no fur, were malnourished, and showed every bone in their four-pound bodies. They were said to be poodle-mixes, but they didn't resemble any poodles I'd ever seen. They were so different from the kind of dog I wanted that, although I felt sorry for the puppies, I didn't even consider adopting one of them.

The SPCA had two rows of cages stacked along a hallway. I worked along one side of the cages, giving dogs their daily exercise. One day, I felt a tap on my shoulder. I looked around, thinking it was someone who wanted information about one of the dogs, but no one was there.

When I put back the dog I had been walking, I felt another tap on my shoulder. This time, I saw that one of the ugly pups had reached his paw through the cage to touch me. I laughed and talked to him, all the while thinking he wasn't what I wanted. After all, I absolutely would not have a male dog.

Donna's Abbie

Every time I passed the cage, this puppy would scream, holler, claw, and try to bite his way out to reach me. His insistence made me wonder if God was trying to tell me something. I decided the message must be that I was spiritually connected with this litter, so I decided to adopt one of the female pups from it.

On the day when I was supposed to bring my new puppy home, she still needed to be spayed, so I couldn't take her yet. All that night, I dreamed about the boy dog who had so steadfastly tugged at my heart. The next day, when I took the female out of the litter to finish the adoption, the pup who had wanted to be with me so badly stared at me with a sad, betrayed look.

At that moment, I noticed that the puppy was now wearing a new pink identification card on its collar. Much to my amazement, the "male" dog had been reclassified overnight as a female. She'd been sexed wrong at receiving!

I rushed to the desk to explain that I'd almost adopted the

wrong puppy. I was crying by the time the staff accepted my story, and we switched adoption papers.

Today, Abbie is a certified therapy dog who works with hearing-impaired children and rehabilitation patients. In 1998, Abbie was chosen as Delta Society's Regional Therapy Pet of the Year.

I can't believe that I nearly missed out on having the best dog ever. I truly believe that divine intervention took place. This experience taught me to listen better to my heart and to God. And I'm grateful for what Abbie knew all along: We are two souls who were meant to be together.

Meditation

Has an animal ever chosen you? How has an animal been a vehicle for furthering your ability to listen to life's messages? Have you ever prayed for help and then let go of your attachment to the results? What happened?

All in the Family

Anabela Guerreiro
Mississauga, Ontario

*W*e lived in São Paulo, Brazil, in a high-rise building. Several cats inhabited the garage of this building, and more arrived each day.

One day, a new arrival got my attention. My husband, Manuel, immediately fell in love with him, too. This brown-and-white short-haired cat with penetrating blue-gray eyes was different from the other cats; instead of being fearful, he came right over to us. Due to his small size, I named him Niko, which in Brazil means "something small." Even though there were lots of other people and cats around, we connected so fully with Niko that people often asked if he was mine. I would answer, "No, not yet!"

We thought that our twelfth-floor apartment was too small for us to live comfortably with an animal, so each day I went down to the garage to spend an hour feeding Niko and giving him attention and love. When I finished, Niko would follow me to the elevator as if he were my shadow. He'd stand and watch as the door closed and the elevator took me away.

Our family finally decided that, despite our tiny apartment, we had to adopt Niko. We went to the pet store and bought everything we might need. This time when we called Niko from the garage, we opened the elevator door and he went right in without hesitation.

Then he followed us to his new home. In the first days after Niko's arrival, all this cat wanted was hours of attention and affection. Manuel would let Niko stay on his lap as long as the cat wanted to be there.

When Niko showed up in our lives, Manuel was suffering from a depression that probably sprang from a frightening experience he'd had: as he sat in his car at a traffic light one day, a young boy pointed a gun at his head. After this incident, Manuel lost interest in everything he used to enjoy — friends, books, life in general. The only thing he looked forward to at the end of the day was playing with Niko.

Anabela's Niko

When we took Niko to the vet, he estimated that the kitten was about six months old. Based on this information we decided to give Niko the birth date of October 7.

While the process of adopting Niko was going on, we were also applying for something else we wanted very much: a visa to emigrate to Canada. São Paulo is like any other huge city with lots of problems; our greatest concern about staying there was the growing violence and uncertainty regarding the future. We'd thought about leaving the city for many years, but after the gun incident with Manuel, we knew we didn't want to be insecure or to feel like we were prisoners in our own home.

The decision to leave was very hard to make. After all, we love

Brazil and have many good friends there. But after Manuel's stressful experience, we finally got the courage to apply for a Canadian visa. We received it quickly, on October 7 — Niko's first birthday.

When it came time to move from Brazil to Ontario, people thought we were crazy for insisting on taking our cat with us. But we always knew that wherever we went, Niko would go, too. Niko played such an important role in Manuel's recovery from depression that we wouldn't ever want to be without him. A good friend of ours offered to keep Niko, but we could have left everything behind except this cat. We cherish every day with him. Leaving him was something we wouldn't even consider; Niko was already part of our family. Sometimes I think that, since life didn't give me a child, it brought me this lovely cat instead. Who knows? Mother Nature has her secrets!

As it turns out, Niko has kept a little bit of the Brazil we love alive for us. He has the good humor and happiness of the Brazilian people. He doesn't ask too much from life; just to be loved is enough. Niko is our Brazilian angel. Bringing him with us was the best thing we could have done. Today is a gift, and Niko is part of that gift.

We thank God for Niko, and we know that our bond with him will last forever. God gave animals a special power to captivate and never disappoint us. We thank Niko for what he has brought into our lives.

That Special Someone

Doris Rouse
Ray City, Georgia

In 1988, I stopped at a roadside fruit stand, where I noticed a tiny, part-Siamese kitten. Her eyes were crusted and fleas crawled all over her. She looked almost lifeless.

I asked the owner of the fruit stand if the kitten belonged to him, and he said she didn't. He wanted me to take her home. I was reluctant to do so because my husband, Talton, had said we absolutely couldn't adopt one more stray cat. But as I was leaving, I took another look at that pitiful little kitten and had to go back to get her. I decided to call her Buffy. When I brought her home, I told Talton that I'd find someone to adopt her and would only keep the cat until she grew healthier.

However, by the time Buffy was well enough to leave our home, she loved my husband. An ornery cat with everyone but him, she'd have nothing to do with the other cats or with me. Buffy could get Talton to do anything she wanted. For example, he had to scratch her back while she ate, or she'd refuse food. She wouldn't drink unless he held the water in his hand. Buffy managed to train my husband well, and he both spoiled and loved her very much. It was clear that she was not going to another home.

A couple of years after Buffy came to live with us, Talton was diagnosed with cancer. Soon he became too sick to pamper Buffy as he had in the past. I tried to take over, but she didn't want me to do the things he had done.

As his condition worsened, Talton became bedridden and Buffy stayed in bed with him day and night. He always kept one hand on

Doris and Talton's Buffy

Buffy. The last time he tried to move his hand was to pick it up and rest it on Buffy. He was too weak, so I placed his hand on his friend for him. Then they were both content. A few days later, Talton lapsed into a coma and died at home in his bed with Buffy by his side.

After Talton's death, Buffy crawled under the bed and wouldn't come out for days. She never again got on top of that bed. For weeks, I tried to coax her out and sometimes managed to pull her from underneath the bed, but she always ran back and hid. Then one day a repairman came to install a new meter box in the bedroom and Buffy went wild. She ran around the room, bouncing off walls and windows, until I opened a door and let her outside. From that point on, she spent almost all her time on the roof. Occasionally I'd catch her and bring her back inside, but she'd immediately run outside again. About a year ago, Buffy decided she'd move back into the house but she still won't go into the bedroom where Talton died.

Although my husband and Buffy had only three years together, they developed a strong bond, and he loved her more than any cat he'd ever had. I believe that Buffy helped prolong his life. Because of their special relationship and the fact that she was such a comfort to him until the very end, I had Buffy's picture painted on the head-stone at Talton's grave. Now everyone who visits the cemetery knows that Buffy was a special part of my husband's life, as he was of hers.

Meditation

What promises have you and an animal made to bring comfort and joy to each other?

Matchmaker, Matchmaker, Make Me a Match

Ellen Moshenberg
Arad, Israel

I moved to Israel with my cat, Shahama, and became a volunteer in a small poor town where I helped a social worker assist her elderly clients. I was also translating Hebrew for a volunteer art teacher in a junior high school. Shahama and I went everywhere together, but bringing animals along was against the rules of the volunteer program so I had to be a bit sneaky about doing it.

One night, a group of volunteers and I were invited to take a midnight tour of the local ceramics factory, and I brought Shahama with me. I was holding her in my arms when the factory's night-shift manager, who was our tour guide, came over and took her from me. He then conducted the entire tour while holding Shahama in his arms. His tenderness with my beloved pet impressed me.

Ellen's Shahama

Soon afterward, we started dating. Now we've been married for twenty-three years. Shahama, our little matchmaker, lived with us for twenty-one of them.

Meditation

Could an animal have been sent as a messenger to help you discover something important about a potential love interest?

Cindy Finds Our Friends

R. Dale Hylton
Canby, Oregon

*W*hen I took a new job, I knew I'd have to make provisions for Cindy, my miniature platinum poodle pal. I was eventually able to find an apartment with two roommates, John and Tom, who helped care for Cindy when I had to travel.

When John or Tom walked Cindy, they began to notice that she showed a preference for certain people. Others she deliberately avoided. We discussed this and concluded that Cindy might be very perceptive in judging character.

So when we went on walks with Cindy, we began to stop and chat with people she liked. Invariably, they turned out to be people we liked and wanted to get to know better. Then we started chatting with people Cindy avoided. We never found anyone, if we talked long enough, who didn't have a bad attitude about something. Usually they were negative enough that we wouldn't have wanted them as friends. We eventually agreed that we'd let Cindy be the final arbiter in the selection of people we would have as mutual friends.

R. Dale's Cindy

It was an excellent decision. Cindy even helped Tom find a wonderful woman who became his wife. As long as we depended on Cindy's innate judgment of character, our close circle of friends remained unparalleled.

Mr. Kitties, the Grief Counselor

Lisa Altieri-O'Brien
Uniontown, Ohio

When I was twenty-two years old, I found a tiny kitten on the beach while vacationing on the Outer Banks of North Carolina one summer. The kitten was in poor condition, and I couldn't bear to leave him to die, so I used some of my vacation money to take him to a vet on the island.

This sickly kitten turned out to be a beautiful, long-haired, orange angora cat. I named him Puddy. I was fortunate to have Puddy as my baby for two years before he died from respiratory problems that he'd developed as a kitten.

Words can't explain my heartbreak on the night Puddy died. My mom held on to me as we both cried. She was the one who had taught me to love animals, so she understood what I was feeling. I swore I'd never get another cat after Puddy.

Over the next couple of years, I dreamed of a black cat several times. I even dreamed that I watched my Puddy run into a cat carrier and come out as that black cat. I didn't know what this meant, if anything. While I was in college, about a year after having these dreams, I came home from work one morning at three o'clock. As I entered the house, a black cat dashed past me and ran right into the house. I was startled and put him outside.

The following morning, I was in the bathroom on the second

floor and heard a meow. I opened the window and was surprised to find the same black cat from the night before sitting on the roof and staring at me. I reached out and picked him up, then put him outside again.

The next day, the black cat appeared on the fire escape at my bedroom window, three floors up from the ground. He was crying for me to let him in. That's when I finally accepted that this cat was determined to adopt me. So I kept him and named him Mr. Kitties.

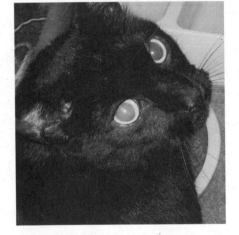

Lisa's Mr. Kitties

Little did I know that Mr. Kitties would soon become my only friend. He was there for me when my mom died two weeks before I graduated from college. I cried and sobbed endlessly over losing her. Mr. Kitties stayed with me every minute. He paced nervously whenever I lay on my bed to cry. I could tell he was upset that I was upset, so I would get up to feed and play with him. He slept in my bed every night and followed me around the house all day. Because of him, I was able to keep going through my grief — and even to laugh sometimes, feeling Mr. Kitties's warmth and love and knowing that I wasn't alone.

Mr. Kitties helped me more than anyone. It's as if he knew, that night when he showed up at my house, that he had to get into my heart to help me through the rough times ahead.

Meditation

As you reflect on the circumstances under which you met an animal, are you wondering if this special friend was meant to be with you at exactly the right time?

CHAPTER FOUR

Angel Animals Heal Hurting Hearts, Bodies, and Minds

Life always bursts the boundaries of formulas.

— Antoine de Saint-Exupéry

*A*nimals seem to be God's natural healers. In *The Healing Power of Pets*, Dr. Marty Becker, DVM, explores many health benefits of having animal companionship. He cites studies showing that people who have animal companions also tend to have lower blood pressure, less stress, and fewer bouts of depression or feelings of isolation than people who don't have animals. And those are only a few of the ways in which animals improve people's quality of life. Dr. Becker writes, "Our beloved pets are like vitamins fortifying us against invisible threats: like seat belts cradling against life's crashes; like alarm systems giving us a sense of security. Taken together, the healing power of pets is powerful medicine indeed."[1]

The stories in this chapter bring home the point that God sends us healers with wagging tails, long pink tongues, or furry coats. Perhaps these stories will remind you of animals in your own life who have served selflessly as healing agents for your heart, body, and mind.

Ferrets Are Made of God

Rebecca Stout
Hixson, Tennessee

*M*y son Sean has been diagnosed with the most common form of high-functioning autism. My husband, Scotty, and I never thought we'd see Sean formulate his thoughts and feelings, much less spontaneously communicate them to someone. Yet today I watch Sean soak up things that are normally sensory assaults to a child with autism — all because of a little ferret named Rocky.

When Sean was five years old, he seemed to make a developmental leap. We seized this opportunity to try out animal companionship. Although experts on autism neither recommend nor reject the idea of autistic children having pets, they caution parents to supervise the child's interactions with animals. Autistic children can be physically explosive, whether from joy or anger. We went through a series of pets with varying degrees of success for Sean: beta fish (those colorful little fish found in pet stores that are kept in small bowls by themselves and are easy to care for), frogs, a snake for his older brother, Chet, and a dog. Sean didn't do well with dogs, and dogs were not fond of him. He seemed to still have an impulsive streak that made us cautious about keeping pets in our home.

Scotty longed to have a ferret, and I'd had ferrets as a child and loved them, so one day I decided to bring home two ferret kits.

Although Sean acted disturbed at first, under my watchful eye he began to forge a relationship with these animals. The first time Sean had to be away from the ferrets was a school day. When he came home, he burst through the door, plopped down in front of the cage, and refused to take off his book bag while he stared at the kits for twenty-five minutes, waiting considerately for them to wake up. He was so protective of them in the initial weeks that guests weren't even allowed to look at the ferrets.

Over the months, Sean learned self-control by giving the animals water and food. He mastered the skills of safely holding and playing with them, and he learned not to stick his fingers in their cage. Not a day passed without Sean surprising us with the details he was picking up about how to handle the ferrets.

When the ferrets first arrived, Sean would mimic how Scotty spoke to them and repeat word for word whatever my husband said. But then Sean made an important advance in his development: He began to spontaneously speak to the ferrets with his own words and for his own reasons. After a while, he developed a style of touching and relating to them.

On Valentine's Day, we surprised Sean by taking him to a local ferret shelter. When the woman who ran the place showed us a ferret named Rocky, Sean asked if this ferret was "special." The woman assured him that Rocky had come to the shelter dying, and it was a miracle that he'd lived at all. Rocky had overcome many things and, like my son, was a survivor. We took Rocky home that day.

Soon Sean was brushing Rocky's fur even though he couldn't stand having his own hair brushed. He learned the names of his ferrets' foods. Sean also learned how to wash the cages and trays, change the water bottles, scruff the ferrets (hold them up by the skin and fat on the back of their necks — a safe form of discipline), and take them to the vet.

Rocky moved more slowly than the other ferrets, and he was gentler with Sean, so Sean responded to him well. Before long, Sean and Rocky had become the best of pals. The close bond between them became the bridge Sean needed to achieve a dream.

Sean loved baseball and enjoyed watching his older brother play. He often worked the scoreboard with me as I announced the game. He learned the rules and thrived on them. Eventually he expressed a dream to play baseball himself.

We tried having Sean join a special league, but that didn't work out well for him. He needed the rules to be exact, and this league didn't have

Rebecca's son Sean and Rocky

rules he could accept. With great reservations, we decided to let him join the regular league. There was no doubt that Sean could play well. But there was great doubt about whether he'd be able to hold up under the social pressures, let alone tolerate all the touching, noise, and sensory assaults involved in playing ball with other children.

When Sean first showed up on the field, he was too scared to go over and talk to the "normal" children. We'd brought Rocky along, and I got the idea to put the ferret in Sean's arms. His face and body instantly relaxed as the ferret's love helped my son become less rigid.

We walked up to the other boys. They greeted Sean with big grins and "wow"s. Sean didn't say a word. He just shook his head, yes or no, and hugged Rocky tightly.

Pretty soon, Sean was able to sit in the dugout. Before long, he was playing ball with the team. Of course, Rocky was right there in the stands rooting for him.

Fate seemed to decree that having a ferret for a mascot was lucky. Sean's team went all the way in the tournament and won the championship that year. The entire experience was the most positive in Sean's life — and it was all possible because of the love and friendship he found with Rocky.

One day, I listened as Sean held Rocky in his arms, stroking him and talking to him about everything under the sun. Then he asked, "Mommy, what are ferrets made of?" Before I could come up with an answer, Sean thought of his own. "God," he said. "Ferrets are made of God."

And I agreed with him.

Meditation

What animals have you met who were "made of God" and helped you heal enough to take your next steps in life?

The Compassion of Noodles

Judy Tatelbaum
Carmel, California

"Compassion" should be my dog Noodles's given name. A female black Labrador–mix, she has an extraordinary sense about when people are in need and moves toward them with all the love she can muster. People always know that Noodles cares about them by the loving look in her soulful brown eyes.

I first noticed Noodles's compassion when she was a puppy. I gave a party for thirty volunteers from our local AIDS project. Noodles spent the evening going back and forth among the three people who were ill with AIDS.

When I took her to the HIV/AIDS support group I lead, Noodles spent two hours every week lying on various clients' laps. If a member of the group seemed particularly upset, she would stay with that person all evening. Noodles became my coleader.

Soon Noodles also became my cotherapist. A seventeen-year-old girl, Sally, came to me for psychotherapy. She'd witnessed a very disturbing fatal incident of family violence. I had never before worked with anyone in the immediate aftermath of such a devastating experience.

When Sally arrived at my office, I ushered her toward the sofa. Noodles followed. Sally sat down. Noodles, who isn't allowed on the furniture, immediately crawled up on Sally and lay across her lap

Judy's Noodles

like a warm, furry blanket. I was startled and almost told Noodles to get down, but then I saw Sally smile and pet the dog. Noodles spent much of the session looking up into Sally's face and licking her. Noodles stayed with Sally for the whole hour and for all of her subsequent therapy sessions. Later I found out that Sally had several pets of her own and loved dogs. I was never sure how much I helped Sally, but I knew that Noodles's love and support made a huge difference in the teenager's healing.

Since then, I notice that whenever Noodles sees someone who is in pain, she licks them and stays by their side. She contributes to my clients' recovery in ways that no one else ever could.

A Hamster's Legacy

Ruby M. Hanna
Winnipeg, Manitoba

The first few months in the sixth-grade classroom where I had been newly assigned were absolute chaos. Oh, how I longed for the old days in my formerly peaceful suburban school. But due to a reshuffling of students, inner-city children from a new housing development were being bussed into our school for the first time.

Playground behavior was like nothing I'd ever experienced, with kicking, fighting, swearing, and bullying being the norm rather than the exception. Inside the classroom, things weren't much better. Some students carried knives to school and threatened anyone at any moment. I watched helplessly as students whacked each other over the head, stabbed other students with sharpened pencils, and bit and kicked until someone had the courage and strength to intervene. A favorite activity among students at the beginning of this horrible school year was to set the restroom garbage cans ablaze. I truly felt as if I were trying to teach in a war zone.

Our faculty used every technique any of us had ever learned to try to get the situation under control and bring an end to this turmoil and confusion. I found myself asking from the depths of my being for God to help me. But it seems to be a universal law that help arrives in unexpected ways. I almost didn't recognize the miracle when it first came.

One day, a sensitive, freckle-faced boy named Teddy brought his hamster, Wee Boy, to school. Wee Boy was a furry blond creature with a twitching nose and soft brown eyes. I asked Teddy to talk to the class about how to care for hamsters. To my amazement, a distinct change occurred in the room as Teddy talked. It actually became quiet and peaceful. We gathered in a circle on the floor, and the students became attentive. Their interest turned into excitement as each child shared a few minutes of loving tenderness with the hamster. Even the knife-wielders' faces softened when they gently cuddled this vulnerable little fellow in their arms.

An idea was born.

The next morning, I arrived at school with six hamsters in shiny red cages. I lined them up on the cupboard walls and placed around them pictures and books about the care and feeding of hamsters. When the students filed in, I enjoyed watching their awe and disbelief over the new development. They wanted to know, "Do the hamsters really belong to us?"

Once again, we formed a circle on the floor — a practice I began to call the Magic Circle — and got acquainted with our new pets. My students voted on names, such as Mandika Warrior, Cuddles, Sammy, and Blondie, according to the hamsters' colorings and personalities.

In the next few weeks, the students read library books and learned how to feed the hamsters, give them water, and clean their cages. They were so involved in this new project that they began arriving before the morning bell to cuddle and talk with their new hamster friends. At the end of each day, they were reluctant to leave. Each student wanted just one more minute with the animals.

Before long, I noticed that the children were dressing better without my making any suggestions. They started wearing shirts with deep front pockets so that they could cradle a sleeping hamster inside them. The same hands that had whacked at and stabbed classmates were now gently holding their tiny, vulnerable hamster friends. The unspoken rule was: We shall not harm hamsters. Many of the students even convinced their parents to adopt a hamster at home.

Meanwhile, Teddy had decided to let Wee Boy live in our classroom with the other hamsters. One morning, much to everyone's surprise, Teddy's hamster had a bundle of nine babies. Everyone was shocked; we'd all thought Wee Boy was a male! That day, the librarian received thirty-two requests from our classroom for books about reproduction. The questions and discussions seemed endless.

When the babies were old enough, I released them from their cage and they scurried across the carpeted floor, running from student to student. The classroom erupted with playfulness, laughter, joy, and camaraderie. The baby hamsters had rallied our students into a community.

Parents, fellow staff members, and visitors were amazed at the behavioral changes they saw in my classroom. Other teachers started to incorporate the Magic Circle program. Their students began to arrive at school on time so they wouldn't miss this introduction to the day. They often returned from recess and requested a Magic Circle meeting to solve playground problems. As they shared their feelings more openly, the circle closed tightly, protecting children who were expressing deep sadness over their losses of pets or their parents' divorces.

Our morning Magic Circle meetings began to elicit ideas for

making our school more interesting and exciting. Suggestions included plans for an outdoor education program and a trip across Canada. Soon we were going camping as a class and cooking stew over bonfires. In a heart-stopping moment on one of these trips, a youngster whose vocabulary had mainly consisted of four-letter words balanced stew on a paper plate in the rain and said with shining eyes, "This is the happiest time I've ever had."

Before coming to my classroom, most of my students had never visited an airport, eaten in a restaurant, traveled outside the city limits, been in a boat, boarded a train, or flown on an airplane. But during that special year, we visited historic sites far from Winnipeg — and, for the first time, they splashed and swam in the Atlantic Ocean. Sometimes in my dreams, I relive these scenes and recall the joy and light in faces and hearts that had once been closed, dark, and angry.

Some of my former students keep in touch with me. When we celebrate together, we always remember Teddy's hamster, who started us on a journey from hate and fear to love and friendship. A tiny hamster breathed on our cheeks and left her paw prints on our hearts.

Meditation

Has an animal been the catalyst for transformation and healing in your life? As you look back on times when you moved from lovelessness to feeling loved, did an animal help you make that transition?

Kitten Launches a Law Career

Mary Margaret McEachern
Wilmington, North Carolina

I have taught numerous Sunday school classes at my church about God's purpose for animals and my belief that they join us in heaven. As an Animal League Defense Fund attorney in my area, I devote much of my practice to protecting the rights of pet owners. I feel that one of my purposes on this earth is to force the law to evolve into considering animals as true family members, which they are, and not merely as property. I have written legal briefs on animals, citing the Bible as authority. I find animals to be my favorite clients. They never argue, say bad things behind my back, or second-guess me, yet they are eternally grateful.

I have loved animals all my life, but it was a special cat named Kitten who saved my life and launched me on the path to becoming an "animal lawyer."

I am an avid marathon runner. When I was in law school, I needed a release from stress, and running seemed the perfect activity. But I was running too much, almost to the point of obsession. I was also suffering from an eating disorder. I had literally stopped eating, and was taking in nothing but carrot and vegetable juices and other liquids designed to give me nutrients. I had lost a phenomenal amount of weight in a very short period. I studied until all hours of the night and was sleep-deprived. All of these factors became a deadly combination for my health and well-being.

One summer, my right lung collapsed. The medical term for this condition is "spontaneous pneumothorax." In my case, the cause was partly my overtraining and partly congenital. My lung collapsed five times in the course of one year.

I lived alone in my apartment while in law school, and with my lung doing unpredictable things I was truly afraid I'd die in my sleep. Surgery was inevitable, but that scared me, too.

Mary Margaret's Kitten

Halfway through this ordeal, I adopted Kitten. She literally changed my whole outlook on life. Just having another heartbeat in the apartment with me calmed my fears. She developed a wonderful habit of sleeping with her little paws wrapped around my neck in a loving embrace every night. She was like a drug as she lulled me to sleep.

Kitten would begin our nighttime ritual by rubbing her paws on my head, giving me the most wonderful massage. This head massage was accompanied by the sound of her deep, satisfying purr. She would eventually massage her own little self to sleep. As I lay with her paws around me, I listened to her breathing and heartbeat and felt her warmth. This combination had a narcotic effect on me.

When spring came, I opted for having surgery so that I could resume my training. After each of my two operations, Kitten gravitated to the painful area and made it feel better. There were times, I must admit, when she was the only reason I wanted to continue living, as I had become extremely depressed from not being able to do my workouts. Gradually, my surgical scars healed and I have been able to compete in two marathons since the operations. I continue to feel strong, and I am now happily married to Kitten's adoptive father, Tommy.

Kitten sleeps with us every night, and she still loves to massage my head. I fall asleep with her touch and awaken to it in the morning.

Meditation

Is there an animal who brought healing comfort to you or others when God couldn't get through any other way?

Bon Jour Helped Mary
Have a Good Day

Linda L. Nickerson
Fallbrook, California

*W*e often take our miniature horses, Moon Shadow and Bon Jour, to nursing homes. Owing to their small size and gentle nature, we can safely lead them right into the rooms of bedridden patients, giving them much-needed environmental enrichment. Having a little horse in their room really thrills them. But the most touching moment of our lives came when we were showing our minis at the Lane County Fair in Eugene, Oregon, where we used to live.

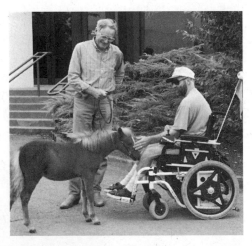

Linda's Bon Jour and friends

A caretaker of a very disabled young woman approached us and asked if we could let her patient, Mary, pet one of our horses. We brought our weaning filly, Bon Jour, over to Mary's wheelchair. Mary was partially paralyzed and totally blind, but our little horse seemed to sense the need to be extra careful as she put her head into Mary's lap. The young woman slowly ran her hands and fingers all over Bon Jour's velvety muzzle, around her nose and ears, over her closed eyes, and through her mane.

Then with tears in her eyes, Mary quietly said, "Thank you. I've never seen a horse before and now I have."

Needless to say, there wasn't a dry eye in the area. We could not have chanced bringing a full-sized horse that close to Mary. Something might have spooked a big horse, causing him to bump and possibly injure the young woman. But with a mini of only about fifty pounds, the encounter was totally under control. And we all had an experience we'll never forget.

Meditation

When have healings been brought to you by the smallest creatures? Has a tiny animal ever been the vehicle for big blessings?

PART TWO

WISDOM

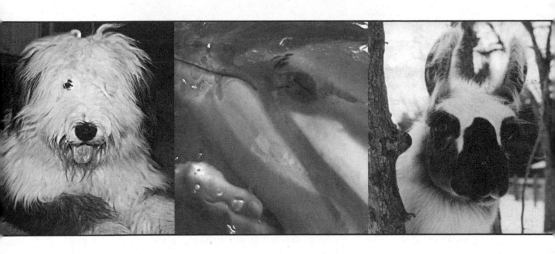

There is no life apart from living things,
and each life sustains another;
You experts ought to think about this,
and care for all life with love.

— Kabir, from *The Bijak*

CHAPTER FIVE

Are Prayers Answered?

Dear God,
Thank you for the baby brother but what I prayed for was a
puppy.

— Joyce (*Children's Letters to God*)

uddles, our black-and-white kitty, sits on the window ledge looking out at squirrels skittering by and birds swooping down from the sky. Only her white whiskers twitch as soft spring air kisses her face. Occasionally her tail, with the tip looking as if it has been dipped in vanilla ice cream, waves back and forth charting the movement of a neighbor out for a jog or a mother pushing her baby's carriage on the sidewalk. Nothing disturbs this cat. No muscles move as she rests with her paws tucked under her chest. This cat has mastered the art of solitude and quiet meditation.

Watching Cuddles sit still and contemplate life outside her window brings to mind a question: Do all creatures have the ability to tune into and connect with the Divine?

Andrew Newberg, MD, Eugene D'Aquili, MD, and Vince Rause, in

Why God Won't Go Away: Brain Science and the Biology of Belief,
write about the theory that there is a neurological basis for our
human desire for God:

> The expansive neurological distance between the human brain
> and the nervous system of a worm is difficult to measure, but
> it is not infinite. The difference is primarily a matter of com-
> plexity. Neurologically speaking, in fact, complexity is primar-
> ily what separates the worm from the toad, the toad from the
> chimp, and the chimp from, say, Stephen Hawking.[1]

Their findings, using brain scans of Tibetan Buddhists meditating and Franciscan nuns in deep prayer, show neural activity in the
left parietal lobe when people have "peak," or transcendent, experiences. They believe their studies prove the existence of a higher reality, described by mystics throughout the ages — what some might
call interconnectedness or union with God.[2]

So what happens in animals' brains when they hear the sounds
of prayer, hymns, or chanting? Is a cat purring or praying? Do animals also slip naturally into meditative states? In the coming years,
will scientists discover that when a cat, dog, or ferret curls up on
your lap while you pray or meditate, your pet's brain waves also register bliss, transcendence, or enlightenment?

The stories in this chapter deal with the role of prayer in the
lives of both humans and animals. They offer intriguing insights into
how prayerful minds and hearts bring comfort and even miracles.

Amazing Grace and the Dolphin

Sierra Goodman
Miami, Florida, and Costa Rica

The dolphin swam back and forth along the shore. She finally moved into shallow waters, beaching herself. We reached her and tried to stop her from rolling onto the rocks.

At about 9:00 that morning, at the Delfin Amor Eco Lodge in Drake Bay, home of the Dolphin Foundation of Costa Rica, we'd received a call from the Costa Rica Adventure Divers, another lodge in the area. They'd asked us to help them with a dolphin. Now our marine biologist was calling another organization, the Marine Stranding Center in San José, Costa Rica, to ask for advice on how to handle the situation. They told him that we should get the dolphin into a saltwater pool. The Marine Stranding Center would send veterinarians out later in the day to determine if the dolphin was sick.

Luckily, Drake Bay Wilderness Resort had recently built a seaside cement pool filled with ocean water. We fashioned a sling out of an old sheet and cut holes for the dolphin's pectoral fins. Carefully we placed her in our boat, and soon we had her in the pool. Since dolphins don't easily comprehend enclosed spaces, we held on to her and kept her from swimming into the walls.

As we waited for the vets to arrive, we checked out the dolphin for identification and verified from her beautiful gray-and-white markings that she was a striped dolphin. In all of the tours we had conducted from our facility, none of us had ever seen this species. They tend to live in very deep waters far from shore.

As we held the dolphin and talked to her, Alecia Evans, a volunteer at Delfin Amor, began to hum "Amazing Grace." We didn't know then that this much-loved hymn and prayer would become a theme song for an adventure and inspire us to name the dolphin Grace.

Grace responded positively to our humming. She even went so far as to put her snout into our hands. As we continued to sing "Amazing

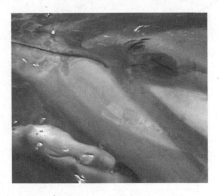

Sierra's Grace

Grace," her breathing relaxed; she even nudged us with her pectoral fins every time we stopped serenading her.

Because of their inability to get a flight and their car breaking down, it turned out that the veterinarians from the Marine Stranding Center weren't able to get to us and help Grace. Throughout the day and night, the staff, guests from Delfin Amor and other resorts, and volunteers from scuba diving clubs took turns holding and singing to Grace. They counted her breaths and heart rate every half hour. Everyone who entered the pool felt a special closeness with Grace. She seemed to understand that we were trying to help her. Though she occasionally stretched, she didn't use her extreme power to try to get free.

We kept Grace afloat, giving her all the love we could. Right before our eyes, her skin began healing from the cuts and scrapes she'd gotten while trying to beach herself. We were amazed to see her body recover so quickly.

People came from all over Drake Bay to see Grace. Many children got into the water with her. For most of them, this was their first opportunity to see a dolphin up close. They all asked questions about dolphins, and we happily answered them. We explained that pollution is harming the oceans, and that sonar testing for oil confuses and damages a dolphin's delicate sonar system. The children listened intently. Perhaps some of them will become marine biologists because of their encounter with Grace. It would be just one of the many gifts she left with us.

By the next morning, it was clear that Grace's fate was up to us.

Some of the children who had visited Grace the day before returned. They told us that they'd prayed during the night for their new dolphin friend. We told the children that their prayers had helped; Gracie was still alive.

When high tide came, we got Grace into the water. But she wouldn't swim, so we swam her out farther and farther from shore, keeping her supported and above water. We'd let her go, and she'd sink straight down. We'd lift her back up and shout: "Come on, Grace. You can do it. Find your pod. COME ON!"

Those of us who were close to Grace watched as she made the decision to swim. We tried to follow her, but she doubled back and swam for shore close to rocks where we couldn't go. Then she turned again to the open ocean. She swam back and forth several times as we called out: "We love you, Grace. Please go home."

Then Grace swam past us for the last time. We watched and cheered until we couldn't see her anymore.

Later, we talked about all the things Grace had taught us. For example, she was a master at getting people to work together. It took the cooperation of four hotels in this area to save her life. Grace also brought to light the need for better stranding and rehabilitation facilities for marine mammals in Costa Rica. And she launched our program to educate local children about cetaceans.

Grace caused us to become more committed than ever to teaching others about dolphins by taking our guests and visitors to experience dolphins and whales in their natural habitats. We believe that people will be touched at seeing them wild, free, and up close.

Perhaps dolphins and whales speak for themselves in the only way they know: by sending a messenger, such as amazing Grace, out of the sea to our shores. Perhaps we only need to listen to their prayers.

As the hymn says, "Amazing grace, how sweet the sound."

Meditation

Has an animal come to you who needs your help for survival? What did this teach you about the interconnectedness of all life? Would you like to try singing a sacred hymn to an animal?

A Meditating Angel Dog

Paula Timpson
Stonybrook, New York

I awoke early one morning with the cool air inviting me to meditate. As I sat on my living room couch, I felt my small American white Eskimo dog, Fritz, lying nearby. His sighs told me that he was right where I was, relaxed with God and at peace, not wanting anything.

When I was finished meditating, I peeked at Fritz. He looked like a true angel, all pure and white as coconut. His paws curled underneath his chest looked like tiny wings. His chin rested on the ground. His eyes were closed. I smiled at the sweet, loving look on his face.

Paula's Fritz

Then I remembered that, the night before, I'd felt lonely and filled with a deep longing as I looked out at the moon and stars. Fritz had run over to me and nudged his wet nose under my hand until I felt better. Then he'd left me and gone back to sleep.

This morning as he joined me, a meditating angel dog, I thanked God for the strong love that has grown between Fritz and me over the years.

Meditation

Would you like to try meditating or praying with an animal nearby or on your lap?

A Moose Messenger

The Rev. Mary Piper
Eagle Point, Oregon

've always believed that my pets would be with me in eternal life. But when my dog Eunice — a shaggy, fun-loving Old English sheepdog — died a couple of years ago in Montana, where we lived at the time, I began to have doubts. Eunice loved the job she had given herself of being my "fuzz alarm," waking me each morning with kisses the minute the alarm went off. Eunice was sensitive, quirky, and loving, and I thought of her as my soul mate during the ten years we spent together.

On the day Eunice died, I took her body outside to be buried, sobbing as I dug her grave. I cried out to God, asking if the animal who had shared my life on earth would be with me in heaven. In my sorrow, I needed a sign that Eunice was with God. At that moment, close over my head, a flock of birds swooped by. I thought, "Oh, that's just a bunch of sparrows." Then I remembered the Bible verse that says, "Not one sparrow will fall to the ground apart from God" (Matthew 12:29).

Okay, that was a pretty good sign.

But I cried again and asked God for a clearer sign. I wanted to see a *mammal*! Just then, even though it was the middle of the day and not a time when such creatures are usually visible in these Montana mountains, a deer walked by.

I had to admit, that was pretty good. But what I really wanted

The Rev. Mary Piper's Eunice

was something that would be too difficult to explain away or chalk up to coincidence: I wanted to see a moose.

I don't necessarily recommend demanding bigger and better signs from God, but God was patient with me that day and very willing to handle my desperation.

After burying Eunice, I went inside. What I didn't realize was that, at the same time, my husband, Harry, had been praying the same prayer; he had also asked to see a moose as a sign that our dog was with God. As he stood outside at Eunice's grave, I heard him calling for me to join him. To our amazement, a big bull moose slowly walked by about sixty yards away from us.

That was clear. I finally got it. I was reassured that my beloved pets will be with me in eternity.

Do animals have souls?

Don't take my word for it. Ask God to show you.

Meditation

Would you like to try Reverend Piper's suggestion and ask about animals as souls and whether they are with God after they die?

The Miraculous Opening of a Heart

Catherine Kirk Chase
Excelsior, Minnesota

*W*hen we took Jasper into our family, he was an eight-year-old, pure white, overweight cat with beautiful gold eyes, a severe shedding problem, and a very distrustful nature. Jasper had good reason for his belief that humans couldn't be counted on. The man from whom we adopted Jasper told us some of the cat's history. He said that Jasper had lived in a series of homes where he'd been neglected, isolated in a cellar, made to stay outside even in severe winters, not allowed to sit on laps or furniture, left alone for long periods of time, and rarely touched. By the time he came to live with us, it was clear that Jasper desperately wanted love but in his difficult life had never learned how to trust or accept it.

Jasper was nothing like the other cats my husband, Lawrence, and I had raised from kittens. The cats in our home are like children. We shower them with love, and they become flexible and patient. Rarely is there an empty lap in sight.

At first, Jasper wanted no part of this love stuff. He remained distressed and often nasty. He'd bite any hand that came near him, hiss at us, and growl at our other pets. Yet the look in his eyes drew us to him. It was as if he wanted us to know that there was so much more to him than he was showing us. We saw Jasper's deep inner beauty and sweetness. So we decided to just give him as much love as he could take. We committed ourselves to his welfare and started patiently teaching him the loving ways of our family.

Lawrence and I did many things to help Jasper feel loved. We gave him nicknames. We developed a special language just for him that we called "jabber babble." We often told him how beautiful he was, with his wonderful long white hair. We let him sit on the sofa.

Catherine's Jasper

Jasper needed to become part of our family and learn to communicate with us, and we needed to learn Jasper's language. So initially we had Jasper ask for food. When he did, we gave him everything he asked for in abundance. This helped him know that in this new home, asking and receiving go together. As Jasper adjusted to being in a loving home, we no longer had to have Jasper ask for food. Gradually he learned not to gorge himself or eat when he wasn't hungry, because there would always be plenty for him. Jasper seemed to equate food with love; we wanted him to know that love is abundant in the world and that he would always receive it from us.

One morning, Lawrence was doing his daily contemplation exercise. He was singing "HU," an ancient name for God that is pronounced like the word "hue" and sung like a chant on the exhaled breath. Singing HU is said to focus the soul on God's love. It is followed by some quiet time for reflection.

As Lawrence sang HU, he felt something jump up on him. Thinking it was one of our other kittens, he reached to stroke the cat's head. That's when he discovered Jasper sitting on his lap, listening to him sing this sacred prayer. Fearing that Jasper would run away, Lawrence sat very still and continued to sing. Then he felt the soft touch of Jasper's face on his lips. It was as if the cat was bathing in divine love. Next, in a truly moving moment, for the first time Jasper allowed Lawrence to pet him.

After that morning, we both began to sing HU to Jasper. Each day, he allowed himself to be loved a little more. Soon, Jasper was even playing — a big step for a cat who had never had reason for expressing joy. Before long, he was letting himself be groomed by our youngest cats with a look of pure bliss on his face.

Love blossomed so fully in Jasper that today he purrs when I pick him up, rub his belly, and kiss him. He follows us around the house and is content to sit with us wherever we are. He's the first to greet us when we arrive home. He talks constantly. Now that he doesn't feel desperate for food, even his extra pounds have fallen away to reveal a sleek body.

I often thank Jasper for being such a treasure. He exemplifies the transformation that can happen when someone accepts love. I have learned much from all the four-legged members of my family, but I have a special place in my heart for Jasper. He allowed me to experience the opening of a heart, and there is no greater joy.

Meditation

Perhaps you'd like to sing HU to animals. See how they connect with this ancient, holy love song to God.

Walk Easy

Sandy Carlson
Woodbury, Connecticut

Sandy's Cuchulainn

Let the lead fall in a slack loop.
Let the dog lead
When you walk.
Dogs read
The landscape
From their ends of slack loops.
They do not forget you
In their yearning to know
Who passed or paused in each moment.
They do not forget you
As they make themselves
A part of the story.
This ancient remembering is
A kind of prayer,
A choosing to know the rocks, the dirt, the trees
That make our lives.
Never pull on the lead
To claim better knowledge.
Do not close this space.
It is not yours to take
Any more than the sun that claims you
When you walk into its rising.

CHAPTER SIX

Why Do Bad Things Happen?

Even God cannot make two mountains without a valley in between.

— Gaelic folk saying

When we were touring to promote our first book, we met a woman at a bookstore who told us a story about her creative and dramatic little cat. This cat experienced what he considered to be a major bad thing in his life. For many years, he had been an "only child." When the woman adopted a dog and brought him home, the cat wasn't ready or willing to adjust to such a terrible turn of events.

This cat was the sort of careful animal who always looked both ways before crossing the street in front of their house. But one day after the intruder had arrived, the cat made certain the woman was looking, then ran into the middle of the street, hurled his body onto the pavement, and stretched his arms out in the form of a crucified martyr. It was as if he were declaring, "I have nothing to live for now. You've destroyed my happy home."

Fortunately, no cars were coming. The woman scooped the cat into her arms and reassured him that he was still her number one son. As time went on, the little thespian realized that his dramas weren't getting the dog thrown out, so he adjusted to the change. Eventually the two animals became the best of friends.

This cat's reaction to adversity seems an awful lot like the way we humans handle life's lemons, doesn't it?

As you'll see in this chapter, it appears that when bad things happen, God sends in the wordless ones — animals who respond with their hearts instead of their minds. These are the creatures who have nothing to say, but so much to give.

Rabbi Harold Kushner, in his book *When Bad Things Happen to Good People,* offers profound answers to age-old questions about why pain and suffering, good and evil exist in this world.[1] The Old Testament of the Bible reflects on these subjects in the following passage:

> Who is he who speaks and it comes to pass
> When the Lord has not commanded it?
> Is it not from the mouth of the Most High
> That woe and well-being proceed?
> (Lam. 3:37–38, NKJV)[2]

Rather than trying to explain why bad things happen, we encourage you to draw your own conclusions after reading the stories and doing the meditations in this chapter. The stories tell of animals and people helping each other to see a bigger picture in situations that at first glance seem unfair or devoid of meaning. These animal and human companions demonstrate that even the most tragic events can become stepping-stones to greater spiritual awareness and deeper peace and happiness. The journeys you'll read about have often required time, patience, and trust before the person or animal could make sense of the experience. But eventually a divine plan has revealed itself and brought comfort.

In the upcoming stories, you'll also meet humans who, while in the midst of heartrending experiences, have become inspired by animals to channel their love into making the world a better place.

Let's start off with a touching story we received from the world-renowned, beloved health-and-fitness coach Richard Simmons. He answered our request for a story with the words: "How can I help you?" Perhaps Richard's experience will help you recognize how, when bad things happen, comfort and understanding come about in unexpected ways.

Spotted Angels

Richard Simmons
Los Angeles, California

*O*ne of the driving forces in my life was my mother, Shirley. She worked so very hard to give me just about anything in the world my heart desired. As I got older, it became my desire to make all her dreams come true.

Yes, I bought her diamonds. Yes, I bought her pearls. I flew her all around the world to visit those great places she'd only seen pictures of in books. Sure, those were all great presents, but the greatest gifts I ever got Shirley were a pair of living, spotted angels.

Oh, I can hear you now: How in the world can Richard actually give his mother angels, and spotted ones at that? He can't get those at Neiman Marcus!

And you're right; you can't get them at Neiman's, but let me tell you, spotted angels really do exist.

What's that? You say you've never heard of them?

Fair enough. But then, please, you have to let me tell you about Rhett and Brent.

I've been a Dalmatian lover for years. In fact, I had six of them, all girls. Their names were Scarlett, Ashley, Marty, Prissy, Pitty Pat, and Melanie. My mother loved visiting me in Los Angeles and playing endlessly with the dogs.

I decided that I just had to have puppies, so one of my girls, Marty, became a mother. Soon I had six baby Dalmatians running all over my house.

Out of those six, there was one special little boy. I named him Rhett. When he was eight weeks old, I took Rhett on a plane ride to New Orleans. I rang the doorbell at my mother's house, and you should have seen Shirley's face when she laid eyes on this puppy. It was love at first "spot."

I saw how happy Rhett made my mom. She went nowhere without him. A year later, it was time for my girl Melanie to become a mother. Soon there were five new puppies. Again, there was one special little boy. I named this guy Brent. And before I knew it, we were on a plane heading to New Orleans again!

Richard Simmons's mother, Shirley, with Brent

I rang the doorbell again, and Shirley's eyes just about popped out of her head. "Another baby for me?" she asked. I don't think I ever saw my mom happier.

Shirley and her two new boys were such a team. Did I tell you how much they liked going to the beauty parlor? No, they weren't going there to get their spots lightened. It was just that wherever Shirley went, Rhett and Brent were sure to go. So when the driver came to pick up Shirley for her ride to the beauty parlor, he was going to have two other passengers as well.

And, oh, they went with Shirley on her trips to the supermarket, too. Hey, they had to be sure that she picked out the right food for supper, you know!

My brother, Lenny, and I could feel a lot safer when Shirley was at home with Rhett and Brent. If anyone came to the front door of the house, they could not come inside unless they had passed the boys' inspections.

I loved my trips home to visit my new extended family. Rhett and Brent would just about knock me down when I got to the house. They were so excited to see me. I loved taking them for walks in Shirley's neighborhood, too. Well, to tell you the truth, it was more like Rhett and Brent were taking me for walks.

Now, we humans know that time takes its toll on all of us. Rhett was no exception. It was so tough watching him slow down, become less energetic. One day we got the bad news: Rhett was suffering from kidney failure. It was not long after that we lost him.

Even Brent realized that things were not quite the same around the house. It was like he got even closer to Shirley. In Dalmatian language, you could hear him telling her, "Shirley, I'll always be with you. I'll always be at your side."

And you know what? He was!

Now, all of us kids feel like our parents are going to live forever. I was no exception. On one trip to New Orleans, in the spring of 1999, I noticed that Shirley wasn't as chipper as usual. She was not feeling well. I'd spent the entire week with her, while Lenny was away at one of the many functions he attends with the Kiwanis Club. He came back on Sunday afternoon, and as I got ready for my flight back to Los Angeles, Shirley asked for one more big kiss from me. And, oh, what a kiss I gave her!

When I got home, a phone call came from Lenny. It was the phone call no child ever wants to receive. Shirley had passed away as I flew back to Los Angeles.

Sadness and tears flooded my soul. The only thing to comfort me then was knowing that Brent had been at Shirley's side. He was in the bed with her as she left this side of life. Brent had kept his promise. He never left Shirley.

After Shirley left us, Brent seemed to slow down. He was still happy to see me when I came home, but he behaved like a much older dog. Not long after that, Brent also passed away.

The spirits of Shirley, Rhett, and Brent still live inside my brother, Lenny, and me, though. And did you think that heaven could be an even more special place?

Well, it is. That's because all the other angels smile when they see this angel, Shirley, throwing a ball and playing fetch with a couple of spotted angels. Yep, those angels with the spots are named Rhett and Brent.

Cassidy and Our Date with Destiny

Karen Lee Stevens
Santa Barbara, California

It was a run-down warehouse, the kind of building you could envision housing old cars or greasy machinery. I looked toward the warehouse and spied a cat sitting on the cold, hard steps of what used to be the entrance to the structure. As I approached the cat and sat down on the step, he trotted over, promptly jumped onto my lap, and started purring.

I didn't know it at the time, but I had just met my destiny.

I could see two old food and water dishes off in the corner, long crusted over from disuse. This cat had to be starving and thirsty. I washed a bowl at an old faucet and filled it with water. I have never seen a cat drink so long and with such enjoyment. With that done and feeling pretty good about myself for helping the poor critter, I said good-bye and promised to come back and see him again soon.

The next day was Saturday, and a rainstorm hit the city with force. As I snuggled contentedly under the covers, my mind went to the kitty I had met the day before. What if he were out in all this rain? What if he were shivering, lonely, and scared? I had to do something. I got up and drove to the abandoned warehouse and, sure enough, there he was, huddled under the eaves of the old building. I strode over, scooped him up, and without a backward glance placed him on my lap in the car and drove home. He made no effort to protest. It was as if he knew I had only the best of intentions toward him.

I didn't really notice it when he was outside, but as I took a closer look at him at home I saw that he had the most beautiful big blue eyes I'd ever seen on a cat. With eyes the color of highly polished sapphires and the depth of the deepest ocean, this cat drew me in with his gaze and we made a deep connection.

I named the cat Cassidy after my teen idol, David Cassidy; I always thought David was (and still is) dreamy. When Cassidy came to me, I really needed the unconditional love he offered so freely. I had recently ended a difficult relationship, and Cassidy helped me feel loved. He quickly became my inspiration and my best friend.

As the months and years passed, Cassidy and I continued to share a special relationship. He was there as I began mulling over the idea of starting an organization to help animals. He was there as I began researching animal rights and animal-testing issues. Every time I learned about another atrocity against an animal, I would sit with Cassidy and gaze into his soulful blue eyes and ask, "Why? Why, in this highly advanced society, is animal abuse happening?" His unwavering gaze and quiet, dignified demeanor helped me continue my research, dig deeper, find answers, and ultimately educate others.

Karen's Cassidy

On the very day that I completed my first book, *All for Animals:*

Tips and Inspiration for Living a More Compassionate Life, Cassidy passed away peacefully in my arms, nestled in his favorite blanket. He was sixteen years old. I have no doubt that he helped me fulfill my purpose of sharing messages of compassion toward all animals. I hope he realizes how important he has been in my journey to help other animals in need.

After all, it was our destiny.

Meditation

When bad things happen, do you ever find yourself being the one who was in the right place at the right time to be a vehicle of transformation? Has a tough situation been a catalyst to bring you more love and comfort?

A Llama with Wings

Lydia Chiappini
Blairstown, New Jersey

*S*everal years ago, my mother and I decided to pool our resources and fulfill a lifetime dream of moving to the country. We purchased some beautiful property and named it Heaven's Gate Farm. We decided to raise llamas there. One day we were visiting a nearby llama farm and met Claude, a mischievous three-month-old llama who was always escaping and getting into trouble. Claude was golden brown and silvery white with huge, lustrous, dark eyes that seemed to look directly into your soul. When Claude sauntered over to us, batted his long eyelashes, and seemed to say, "Take me home," we knew we had to have him.

Claude was delivered to us at weaning. He escaped seven times the first day. Within the next few months, Claude took us through the seasons with much creativity and energy. He tore the screens off windows, ripped open cement bags in the garage, ate all the pansies on the porch, rang the front doorbell with his nose, tried on a ladder around his neck, threw his halter over the fence into the snow, and rolled on the ground like a spoiled brat if I spent too much time chatting with neighbors when we went for walks.

In spite of all his shenanigans, Claude cast a magical spell over our first two llamas, Phoebe and Theo. They suddenly became easygoing in his presence. He became a beloved friend to all of us as we bonded into a family. It was Claude's companionship that helped me through the difficult times when our house partially burned down, my mother had a stroke, and I had to commute four hours each day to a job where I was unhappily employed. I planned for Claude and me to grow old together, and looked forward to enjoying a long life with him.

Lydia's Claude

Unfortunately, this wasn't meant to be. Claude was attacked by a black bear and died in my arms. His loss devastated me. Through my grief, I kept having the feeling that Claude was watching over us.

Losing Claude showed me that life is short and inspired me to quit my job and fulfill another cherished dream. I'd always wanted to teach art in a college and live off the modest income from our farm. After I launched this new way of life, I wrote a book about Claude for children. It was called *The Llama Who Wished for Wings,* and it featured Claude as a llama who wishes to fly with the wings of a bird and has the spirit to do so.

My first Claude book was a big success. I followed it with a story about Claude and a kitten named Vincent, who were real-life friends. *Claude's Wings and Vincent's Toes: A Tale of Two Friends* told about a magical winged llama who adopted an abandoned kitten with twenty-seven toes. Then I wrote and illustrated a book about our farm, *Picotee, the Polka Dotted Llama.*

If it weren't for Claude, none of this would have happened. People who read about Claude tell me they are deeply touched by his story. Some of them are inspired to change their own lives for the better. Others say that when they read Claude's story to their children, it becomes their favorite message of life affirmation.

I feel that our Claude, our angel llama, still looks over us as our special spiritual guardian.

Meditation

Has an animal inspired you to give something special back to life? Has the loss of a loved one brought direction to your creativity, sense of purpose, or desire to serve others?

The Upside-Down Birdhouse

Lorraine Lanzon
Garden City, Michigan

*A*n upside-down birdhouse with a twig-and-grass nest inside sits in a tall pine tree in our backyard. In it, I see four baby birds. "Chips, chips," they chirp constantly, calling for their mother, who is out looking for worms to feed them.

Why is this birdhouse upside down?

In the beginning, the wooden birdhouse was positioned perfectly upright. I enjoyed watching small birds take up residence there, but I got irritated whenever I saw blue jays and blackbirds poking at the eggs inside. Then one day a strong wind blew the birdhouse to the ground. There it lay until days later, when I asked my brother to throw it higher in the tree. He hurled the birdhouse back up into the branches, where it landed upside down with its entrance hole facing the trunk of the tree. This position made the hole invisible to the bigger birds. The tiny space between the front of the birdhouse and the tree trunk, as well as the close branches protecting it on all sides, prevented the big birds from sticking their beaks into the hole.

Now the topsy-turvy birdhouse is in demand among the smaller birds in the neighborhood because it's difficult for large predators to reach into. It has become a refuge, securing eggs and babies in its nest while mother birds are out looking for food nearby. Nature, via a windy "unfortunate accident," has provided the birds with a safe home. Our upside-down birdhouse serves as a reminder that, regardless of initial appearances, what seems to be a bad turn of events may be a good thing when we see the bigger picture.

Meditation

What do pets or animals in nature tell you about why "upside-down" experiences or "unfortunate accidents" might have been exactly what you needed?

Explaining to a Horse How It's All in Divine Order

Lois Stanfield
Chanhassen, Minnesota

When I had to sell my horse, Zeke, it was the hardest thing I have ever done. But the bottom had fallen out of my life, I was moving from Minneapolis to San Diego, and times were extremely tight financially. Zeke was a champion dressage horse and needed to be ridden consistently and cared for properly, and I couldn't afford to give him what he needed.

I searched for the right person to buy and care for Zeke, and found a lovely woman, Kathy, with a teenage daughter who wanted to learn dressage. When I sold Zeke to her, I made her promise that if they ever wanted to sell the horse, she would give me the first right to buy him back. I hoped to provide for his retirement when the time came.

One year after my move, things began to get better for me financially. And the universe seemed to sense that the timing was perfect for Zeke and me to be reunited. To my surprise, Kathy called one day to say that she needed to sell Zeke. Her daughter was leaving for college and had decided to quit riding. Since the daughter had been Zeke's principal rider, the horse would no longer get the exercise and attention he required. My heart was filled with joy at the prospect of having him back in my life — and so much sooner than I ever could have imagined!

As the time neared for transporting Zeke from Minneapolis to Southern California, I called one of the grooms at the stable where he was boarded. Since I was unable to be in Minneapolis myself to prepare Zeke for his journey, I made a request. I said, "I know this might sound crazy, but will you talk to Zeke like he's a five-year-old child? Tell him everything you're going to do and what's going to happen to him during this move. It will be scary. If you don't explain it all to him, he'll think that something awful is happening."

The groom promised that she would have a conversation with Zeke. I felt most grateful that she didn't ridicule or belittle my heartfelt request.

I called the groom the next day to find out if Zeke had gotten off okay. The groom said she had talked to Zeke about his upcoming trip; she explained to him that he was going to get on a truck, and

Lois and Zeke

at the other end of the journey would be his beloved friend Lois. Zeke had never been very affectionate toward this groom, but when she finished this explanation he put his head on her shoulder and nuzzled her. She believed this gesture showed that Zeke had understood what would be happening and was grateful that she'd prepared him.

She added that, when it was time for Zeke to take his journey across the country, he had calmly walked up the ramp of the huge horse van and remained very calm and accepting. It seemed as if he knew where he was going.

Zeke arrived in California at the stable that would be his new home. He was still on the truck when he heard my voice. First he made a little whinny. Then it seemed to register that I was outside waiting for him. That's when he neighed at the top of his lungs. Zeke walked out onto the ramp, and I ran to embrace him.

Our reunion was so happy that I couldn't bear to leave him. I spent the night sleeping in his stall in the barn. And I promised myself and Zeke that we'd never be parted again.

Meditation

Does the example of Zeke and Lois remind you of a time when God prepared you for a change that at first looked like a bad thing? Were you ever surprised (or delighted) to find out that a better future resulted from a change you hadn't asked for?

CHAPTER SEVEN

Are We Mirrors for Each Other?

The world is like a mirror, you see? Smile, and your friends smile back.

— Japanese Zen saying

*W*e've made a discovery during years of sharing stories with people all over the world: observing the animals in your life can help you learn more about yourself. God uses animal vehicles to deliver some almighty spiritual and highly personal messages.

We've concluded that animals often reflect their human companions' values, interests, personalities, and spiritual awareness. Animals also serve as indicators of what people are hiding from the world and themselves. They manifest a person's state of consciousness — flaws and all.

Hang in there with us on this theory because, as you'll see, animal mirrors are a blessing rather than a much-too-revealing embarrassment.

There are many websites devoted to guiding you to select the right animal or breed for your personality and lifestyle. Depending on whether you're friendly, protective, independent, self-assured, consistent, steady, or clever, you'll be advised that a certain animal is more likely to be compatible with you.

Marketers already know a lot about you by the kind of animal companion you've chosen. The University of Oregon conducted research on people who live with dogs, cats, birds, fish, mice, rabbits, or reptiles. The study compared people's lifestyles with the types of pets they choose. Those who share their homes with dogs usually believe in honesty and are more traditionally religious and duty-bound. Cat lovers tend to be independent, just like their pets. People with fish are more optimistic and less cynical.[1] Advertisers analyze these profiles to prepare strategies for how to get you to buy those fancy dog or cat dishes and gourmet pet foods.

People who seek to identify their "animal totems" touch upon this principle of animals as spiritual mirrors. The animal totem is the spirit of an animal species that symbolizes key aspects of a person's spiritual life, appearing in dreams, in visions, and during meditative states. A person's gravitation toward a particular animal totem is believed to come from within the soul, as the animal and human spirits interact with each other for the greater good.

The fact that you're probably attracted to animals who have a bit of yourself in them presents an opportunity for God to help or communicate through your pets. As you will see in this chapter's stories, animals — especially pets — reflect your spiritual blind spots back to you. And this is a good thing.

Spiritual blind spots are the aspects of your personality and spiritual makeup that keep you from becoming your most evolved, loving, enlightened self. They are the needs and desires that you don't, can't, or won't admit you harbor. Recognizing and accepting your spiritual blind spots fosters spiritual growth. The first step toward loving God and others is to love and accept all of yourself. If you don't even know what "all of you" is, how can you love yourself completely?

Throughout your life, you are engaged in a process of becoming all you were meant to be. This healthy wholeness will enable you to accomplish the purpose of your life, yet there are parts of you that remain untouched and untapped. In a natural drive toward becoming complete or a desire to reinvent yourself, you unconsciously draw into your universe people and animals who act out the hidden aspects of what you most fear, love, or hate about yourself.

We've concluded that when animals and humans reflect to one another hidden characteristics, attitudes, or beliefs, they deliver mutually beneficial spiritual messages. Because animals and humans, as sacred companions, can serve as mirrors for each other on life's journey, you have another important tool in your spiritual toolbox.

We received a letter about the concept of sacred companions from Evelyn Alemanni, a member of the board of trustees of the Christward Ministry in Elfin Forest, near San Diego. Evelyn said that, after reading an article about the Angel Animals Network in her local newspaper, she wanted to send us the sermon she'd given at her church. Evelyn says that her congregation offers animal blessings, and animals are allowed to sit in the pews with their human companions for all Sunday services.

An excerpt from Evelyn's sermon, "Sacred Companions," follows.

Sacred Companions

Namasté means "I greet the God in you." Everything God creates has the potential to be sacred. All kinds of sacred companions have in common that they are centers of alignment for the Christ to use.

Evelyn's Benny, Chula, and Sadie

Sacred companions bring out the best in us. They help us discover the higher plan for our lives. They lovingly touch us at the deepest level of our being. They relate to us with openness that knows no boundaries. They inspire us through their character and set examples for how we can live more consecrated lives. Sacred companions are linked to a higher power and, through their alignment to it and to us, bring greater good. Sacred companions can also make us aware of or reinforce spiritual truths.

We invite you to view the animals in your life as sacred companions who serve as spiritual mirrors. As you read this chapter, consider the messages that animal mirrors might be bringing to you when their actions, attitudes, emotions, circumstances, and spiritual qualities reflect your own.

Seeing Parallels, Finding Omens

Grace J. Harstad
Brentwood, California

I was well into middle age when I experienced grief over separation from my cat, Moxie. I'd taken a job in a new city in northern California and, after much searching, I had to rent an apartment that wouldn't allow pets. On a scale of one to ten, with ten being immobilizing depression, my grief was at an eight or nine. Only once in my life, when I'd had to give up my infant daughter for adoption, had I felt a loss this deeply. But the parallels between these two wrenching events, many years apart, were to bring me unexpected comfort and hope.

Only forty-eight hours before I had to move and be parted from Moxie, I called a woman named Vida at the recommendation of a friend. Vida gave sanctuary on her Sonoma Valley ranch to old and abused animals. She said she'd take Moxie, but the cat would have to live in the barn and share a home with a menagerie of horses, burros, goats, geese, dogs, and other cats.

At the end of November, on a rainy, near-freezing day, I made the one-hour drive to take Moxie to the farm. On the way, Moxie clawed out of a brand-new cardboard pet tote and prowled about the car. When we arrived, she fought so hard that, although I was careful not to hurt her, I had to grab Moxie behind the front legs and thrust her into a pet carrier. I placed the carrier on a bale of hay near the open barn door. Then, like a panic-stricken mother abandoning her baby on a stranger's doorstep, I stole away, glancing back at my beloved cat one more time. On my last look back, I saw her sitting upright in her cage, following me with her eyes. All the way home, I worried that Moxie might catch a cold, not get good-enough care, be lonely, or run away. I cried nonstop during the long drive to my new home.

Even though we'd only been together for nine months, I didn't know how I could adjust to life without Moxie. She had arrived unexpectedly as a pretty white stray who appeared on my patio every evening expecting food. I found myself looking forward to her welcoming meow on my return home from work. Soon Moxie had invited herself inside my apartment and transformed my wicker chair into a combination bed and scratching post. Within a few weeks, she connived her way into my bedroom, which I had initially declared off-limits. Then she was on my bed, where I'd once believed cats definitely did not belong. I knew my life had changed irreversibly when I heard myself say one morning, in a squeaky little cat voice, "Bye-bye, Moxie. I'll see you after work."

The evening after leaving Moxie at the ranch, I called to see how she was doing. "Moxie's fine," Vida said. "After I fed her this morning, she scampered up the stack of hay bales to the barn loft." Little did I know then that Moxie had decided to stay in that loft. On her daily rounds, Vida had to deliver food and water by climbing a barn ladder to reach the cat.

On weekends, I brought cat treats and climbed up to the loft, hoping to pet Moxie and comb the snarls out of her once-fluffy white hair. On each visit, Moxie retreated to a ledge beyond a hole in the floor that was inaccessible to humans.

For months, I told everyone how much I missed my cat. Finally a friend said, "Why don't you bring her to live with you? No one will see her."

I mulled over this suggestion for a few days and realized that this decision didn't hinge on rational thought. I would have to listen to my heart.

I returned to the ranch and sat on a bale of hay in the loft. I was prepared to wait as long as it took for Moxie to come to me. As usual, she crouched out of reach. I sat quietly without talking or calling her name as I'd done on earlier visits. Then, with that curious feline telepathy, Moxie apparently sensed that something was different. Within half an hour she padded over, purring as if we'd never been separated. Once we were home, my apartment manager pretended not to see her and allowed both cat and human to stay.

Grace's Moxie

Two years after Moxie and I were reunited, I met my biological daughter for the first time since I gave her up for adoption. Thirty years earlier, when my daughter was ten days old, I had gazed at her one last time through the nursery glass as she lay tucked in her little bassinet. A short while later, I watched as a social worker carried her down the corridor of the unwed mothers' home and out the door to the waiting arms of a stranger. Afterward, I had retreated to my room and sobbed.

This was in 1961, when a young girl did not question social dictates. As an unmarried, middle-class girl, I was not allowed to raise a child. Instead, I was expected to give up the baby for adoption and resume life where I'd left off. The pretense worked for a while, but two decades later I fell to mourning my lost daughter. I began dreaming of a joyous reunion like those I'd seen on television.

Over the years, I had made tentative efforts to search for my daughter, but I was rebuffed by the adoption agency whenever I asked for information. Then, after years passed and attitudes toward adoption secrecy changed, I decided that I had nothing to lose by writing to the agency again. This time the same social worker who had handled my case in 1961 wrote back. She had simultaneously received a letter from my daughter, inquiring about me!

My daughter came from New York for a four-day visit. As we took walks together, drove around the Bay Area, and dined across the table from each other, she remained distant. This thirty-year-old stranger with the same features as the infant behind the nursery glass — this person with whom I'd once shared the closest human tie — set up an impenetrable emotional barricade between us. On the last night of our visit, as we ate together at a restaurant, she told me that she'd only wanted to meet me to satisfy her curiosity and to learn about her family's medical history. "I already have a mother and I do not wish to pursue a relationship with you," she said. As we parted later, she added, "Don't write to me and don't call." She did not turn to wave as I pulled out of my parking space in front of the restaurant, and she walked off to her rental car.

I drove a few blocks, parked my car, and draped myself over the steering wheel and sobbed. Then it all became clear: My daughter was getting even with me. Tonight she had left me the very way I had once abandoned her.

Remembering the day when I sat waiting patiently while Moxie overcame her fears and returned to my lap from her inaccessible perch has helped me understand how deeply wounded my daughter may feel. Perhaps some day, as Moxie did, my daughter will drop her emotional walls. I hope the same spiritual connection that returned Moxie home and caused my daughter and me to write to the adoption agency at the same time will draw us together again.

Meditation

Is there something in your life that you regret? Has an animal's experience ever mirrored your own life lessons? What did the animal's actions show you about your situation?

The Falcon's Return

Janette Warren
Kirkland, Washington

A friend gave me Deepak Chopra's book *The Return of Merlin*, to stir my imagination and create hope for new possibilities within me. Merlin the magician had trained himself, with extraordinary discipline, to create the life he wanted for himself. He developed the ability to transform himself into anything he chose — a stone, a tree — or to disappear into the ether at will. The form Merlin most often used was that of a falcon.[2] To me, this feat of becoming a falcon showed the degree to which anything is possible if the desire is strong enough.

I was nearing the end of Chopra's book, and its powerful images were fresh in my consciousness. As I drove home from the grocery store, I was astonished to see a falcon sitting on a city sidewalk. I sensed that this falcon had been sent to deliver a spiritual message I sorely needed at this time in my life, but I didn't know what it could be. I wanted to get out of the car and investigate, but I had a heavy schedule and needed to get the groceries home.

After putting my groceries away, though, curiosity overcame me. So I drove slowly back down the same street where I'd seen the falcon, looking everywhere for the bird. Suddenly I heard a thump on my car. It sounded as if something had hit the window. I didn't see anything on the ground, so I kept on driving. Then a woman jogger across the street slowed down her pace and gave me a huge smile.

Soon I came to a stoplight. In my rearview mirror, I noticed some commotion in the car behind me. A woman got out of the car and ran up to my window. With a big grin on her face, she asked, "Do you have a pet falcon?"

Like a child who knows that some surprise will be in store, I said, "No-o-o" in a long, drawn-out, questioning tone. She then told me that I'd had a falcon riding on the roof of my car for some time. He had just flown away as she approached me.

Immediately I pulled over, got out of my car, and sat on a porch step near the area where the falcon had flown away. I waited for ten minutes, but the bird never returned.

Touched deeply, I left all possibilities open for the exact meaning of this experience. But the image of Merlin's falcon, followed by a visit from a living falcon, had shown me that anything is possible.

Meditation

Have you missed signs that life is opening up for you in unexpected ways? Are animal messengers being sent to remind you of possibilities?

Simple Gifts

Larry Siegel
Tappan, New York

It was nearing the Christmas holidays, and I will admit to being a humbug about the way we're expected to celebrate them. My father-in-law sent me a present of an audiocassette tape of Shaker melodies, including "Simple Gifts."

"Big deal," I thought ungratefully. I never particularly liked the tune. End of subject — or so I thought.

About two hours later, an associate of mine in the music business called and asked if I happened to have sheet music to — you guessed it — "Simple Gifts." Well, I didn't think I had it but I looked through my files anyway. To my surprise, I found a whole book of Shaker tunes in a volume titled *Simple Gifts*. I didn't even remember having that book!

Okay, okay, I figured, there must be something to this. After all, nobody had ever mentioned that tune to me before, and now twice in one morning this song had come to my attention.

As I began to copy the sheet music for my friend, the tune started to rub off on me. I found myself really enjoying it. The words to the hymn, coming from the Quaker tradition of treasuring the gifts of simplicity and spiritual freedom, seemed special, too — a reminder to be grateful for whatever gifts came into my life.

When my wife came home, she picked up the music and began to whistle the melody. Immediately my two cats, Max and Huki, ran in and started meowing and rubbing against her and each other. Hmmmm. These are pretty quiet cats. Normally they're not at all affectionate toward each other. For nine years, each cat tolerated the other with downright chilliness, a curt nod at the breakfast dish, or the occasional quick scratch-fight. Now, with "Simple Gifts" in the air, Max and Huki were acting as if they had just met and it was love at first sight. Was there something in the message of this sacred melody that caused the cats to be grateful for one another? Incredible!

For hours, Max and Huki stayed in love, meowing, curling up together, and asking for encores by yowling the cat equivalent of "bravo" every time my wife stopped whistling for more than a few seconds. After a while, they quietly slipped off into a closet — together. We wondered momentarily if we should chaperone.

Larry's Max and Huki

It took about a day and a half before Max and Huki returned to their old patterns of either squabbling with or ignoring each other. They never fell back in love again for the rest of their lives. But I will always remember the power that love can bring to a family through the sheer vibration of a beautiful, holy song — a love that was first understood and demonstrated by the feline members of our family and, through them, transmitted to the humans.

What was the message? It's right there in the lyrics:

'Tis the gift to be simple,
'Tis the gift to be free.

Meditation

Have you seen an animal grow in spiritual awareness? Was the animal's lesson similar to your own? When you've had a hard time recognizing life's gifts, has an animal reminded you of your blessings and showed you how to appreciate the simple things?

Forest Family

Harold Klemp
Minneapolis, Minnesota

Our backyard feeder attracts a community of animals. Besides birds we have raccoons, squirrels, rabbits, chipmunks, and deer.

We call the rabbit Stretch. He is very cautious when he comes up to the feed dish, day or night. His only defense is his speed. Fear keeps him alive, and he's grown to be big and old.

Some say the rabbit is a symbol of fear and the deer is a symbol of gentleness. The other day a beautiful doe and a six-point buck came to the feed dishes. I heard a crash in the brush as they approached. The buck came up to the doe, bumped her out of the way, and stooped to the dish himself.

The rabbit sat opposite the dish, watching the buck. They were only four or five feet apart. I was proud of the rabbit's bravery. I told my wife, "The deer hasn't learned anything about gentleness, but the rabbit has learned something about bravery."

The rabbit and squirrels are about equal. Each waits for the other to eat first. If the rabbit's there first, the squirrels get a little pushy and boisterous, but they wait until the rabbit decides to leave the dish.

The most nervy of the creatures is a little chipmunk. He doesn't have any grace at all. When he comes out of the woods, he can hardly see over the top of the grass, but he runs straight at the squirrels. He zips through, coming up behind them, and he scares the living daylights out of them. The squirrels dash up the trees, and the chipmunk flies at the doves next. Pretty soon he's cleared the area and has the dish to himself.

The blue jays are outranked by the squirrels, but they're clever. They'll start making a lot of noise when the squirrels are at the dish. "Danger! Danger!" they scream. And the squirrels all run off into the trees, leaving the dish clear for the blue jays.

This little group makes up a spiritual community. They're learning their little lessons about when to come to the feed dish.

I look at them and think how much they are like people. People divide themselves in one way or another, by age, race, religion, or political affiliation. At the same time they forget we are all God's creatures. What really matters is how people treat each other in the human community.

Meditation

Are there spiritual communities in your backyard that may be reflecting you or the world around you? What lessons in love and power are the animals in nature showing you?

PART THREE

COURAGE

Tyger Tyger burning bright
In the forests of the night:
What immortal hand or eye,
Dare frame thy fearful symmetry?

— William Blake, from "The Tyger"

CHAPTER EIGHT

Angel Animal Heroes

A turtle travels only when it sticks its neck out.

— Korean folk saying

$\mathscr{T}$he world has learned that, in challenging times, ordinary people and animals have the capacity for extraordinarily heroic deeds. With great bravery, animals can act above and beyond natural instinct — running toward danger instead of away from it — to serve as vehicles of divine intervention for protecting and saving lives.

In Buddhism, a bodhisattva is said to be the enlightened deity who voluntarily postpones entrance into nirvana to help others in their quest for enlightenment. We've concluded that there are many bodhisattvas populating the animal kingdom. These are the everyday heroes who serve as search-and-rescue dogs, therapy and service animals, canine police patrols, household pets, or farm animals. We have received many stories about cats, dogs, birds, and other animals who saved entire families from fires, burglaries, and major disasters, often at great risk to themselves. In this chapter, you'll meet animals who shine as examples of courage, bravery, and perseverance.

If the situation presented itself, would you be a hero? Could you be the one God uses to help someone in need? Maybe an animal you know or one you read about in this chapter will bring forth your own heroic nature.

A Dog's Life

Patricia A. Brown
Naugatuck, Connecticut

A lifetime of hurt and anguish was hard enough for me to bear, but when my husband of sixteen years left I could take no more. I decided that it would be easier for me to depart this world. I hoped that death would take me to a less painful place than life had provided.

With those thoughts in mind and no rational emotions, I proceeded to swallow thirty-six sleeping pills, chased down with bottles of champagne. When I finished, there was no turning back. I lay on my bed, feeling the room start to spin around me. My eyes lost focus. My heart began to beat so fast that I thought it would burst. I knew the end of my life was near.

I turned to my faithful dog, a regal rat terrier, and said, "This is it, Gonzo. I'm going."

Gonzo looked at me with determination. I could almost hear him say, "Not on my watch, you're not!"

He then climbed onto my chest and sprawled out. A spray of energy poured from my chest. It felt like Fourth of July fireworks bursting from me into the room in a frenzy of flashes and explosions. At that moment, the lights in the room went out. The television shut off. The clock stopped at 12:04 (and never worked again). Before me was a room full of bright lights, popping and flashing.

I sat up, feeling shocked and dazed. The threat of dying had passed. My heart had calmed to a steady beat. I looked at Gonzo and knew that this angel dog had taken death away.

Of course, I later came to realize that my actions that night had been foolish. In the years since, Gonzo has continued to help and support me in ways that no human has been able to do. Throughout the good and bad, he is always there to give me the hugs and companionship I've needed.

Patricia's Gonzo

For example, my battle with diabetes has been an up-and-down situation. On one occasion, I had a diabetic attack while I was out walking with Gonzo. We were at least a mile away from home, and I was on the verge of losing consciousness. I could hardly stand, but Gonzo kept pulling me along. Everything was a blur. I tried to flag down cars for help, but to no avail. Gonzo never stopped tugging until I was back home, sitting in my easy chair. I must have passed out after I sat down. Hours later, when I awoke, I saw the front door wide open with my precious lifesaver sitting at my feet, keeping guard over me.

Some days, when I've wanted to lie in bed and sulk, Gonzo has kept me going just because I have to get up to walk or feed him. His devotion and unconditional love have been the only therapy I've needed to transform me into the functional and fulfilled person I am today. I love life now, thanks in part to a courageous and determined dog who showed me the true meaning of love.

The Dog Who Knew His Place

David Young
Canton, Ohio

One evening, my son was sitting on my lap as I watched the news. One news story was about a man who broke into a home and tried to carry off a sleeping child. The child had awakened and screamed, causing the intruder to bolt away without him.

I wasn't aware that my four-year-old son had been paying attention to this news story until he woke me up at midnight with his crying. I asked him what had scared him. He said, "Dad, what if someone stole me?"

My son was frightened because he is a very sound sleeper. He must have wondered whether he'd wake up even if someone were dragging him down the stairs.

I asked, "Who sleeps with you?"

"Thor," he said. Thor is our three-year-old German short-haired pointer.

"What would Thor do if somebody tried to steal you?" I asked.

A little smile spread over my son's face. "Eat him," he replied as he hugged Thor, who was in the bed next to him.

"Then what are you afraid of?"

"Nothing," he answered. He wrapped his arms around Thor's neck and went to sleep.

The next morning, I went down to the kitchen and opened the

David's son, Scott, and Thor

back door to let Thor out. But no Thor. I called his name. No response. I went upstairs and found my son sound asleep, with his arms still around Thor.

I called the dog's name. He raised his head and wagged his tail. Then he licked my son's neck and put his head back down on the pillow.

I believe that Thor knew my son needed him. No potty break or breakfast was going to change his determination to stand guard over his boy. I knew that I need never worry about my son's safety while Thor was on guard.

Meditation

Who were your childhood animal heroes? Were there animals sent to protect and safeguard you from real or imagined fears?

Kabootle, Our Rescue Cat

Lauren L. Merryfield
Marysville, Washington

*K*itten Kabootle reached out to me and my daughter, Lynden, from a cage in a pet store. My husband and I had separated only a week before, and now Lynden and I were living single-parent-family-style in our comfortable apartment. When we met Kabootle, a tiny Himalayan, my daughter and I were feeling especially lonely and vulnerable. That day, Kabootle came home with us to meet Melissa, our older cat.

Melissa had diabetes and was getting on in cat years. Eventually, Kabootle decided that the territory in our house had to switch paws from the older to the younger cat. Soon he began taking on the air of The Boss. Several incidents over the years convinced me that part of Kabootle's agenda in claiming his territory involved protecting Lynden and me.

One day as I was getting my mail, the apartment repairman showed up, saying, "You know, I've tried several times to enter your apartment to fix things. My goodness, your cat! I've never seen such a large cat — and that fur and those eyes! I'm sorry, Lauren, but you may have to put him in your room before I can come in."

I laughed and reassured him that Kabootle really was more of a scaredy-cat and would not hurt him. I could understand that the now-fifteen-pound cat, whose lovely blue eyes shone red and menacing in the darkness of our hallway, had taken him aback.

On another morning, I left for work in a hurry, forgetting that I'd put two eggs on the stove to boil. I rushed out the door when my ride came. Lynden had a school holiday and was in her bed sleeping. The smoke alarm in the kitchen began beeping, but no one but the cats was awake to hear it. Kabootle, probably worried by the smell of smoke, the shrill pitch of the alarm, and no sound from Lynden's room, sensed danger.

He padded rapidly to Lynden's bedroom and meowed frantically. Lynden groaned, mumbled, and tried to shove Kabootle off her. But he insistently pawed her face, arms, and hair until Lynden

Lauren's Kabootle

sat up and realized what was happening. She ran into the kitchen to find smoke billowing from the stove, where the eggs and the pan were ruined. She managed to get things under control so that she and the cats were fine.

On another occasion, I was very tired one night and fell asleep instantly. Usually I don't sleep on my back because I have sleep apnea and could stop breathing. That night, I was so exhausted that I didn't notice I'd rolled over on my back. Then I felt Kabootle land on my chest. Evidently the cat had heard my labored breathing and did what he thought would rouse me. It worked.

Another time, when I was very ill, I had lost so much strength that when I tried to get out of bed my legs buckled under me. I fell awkwardly between the bed and the wall with my legs and arms stuck in weird positions. I wasn't quite strong enough to kick or push to free myself.

As I struggled to regain my balance, Kabootle heard me and came running. He took my flailing hand in both of his front paws and pulled with all his might. Of course, the little fellow wasn't strong enough to lift me out from where I was wedged, but his sweet, kind support encouraged me to try again. I twisted my body with great effort and was able to get my other arm free so that I could push on the bed hard enough to crawl out.

We lost Kabootle due to renal failure when he was six years old. I only wish I could have rescued him the way he so often rescued us. I have longed for Kabootle to be rewarded for his bravery, courage, devotion, quick thinking, and love. How blessed we were to have him in our lives and, now, in our memories.

Meditation

When an animal repeatedly rescues others, is this his or her mission in life? How could you get to know more about your purpose by giving service, even under the most difficult circumstances?

Warnings from the Dolphins

Ilona Selke
Starwood, Washington

In late 1980, I found that I had become very attracted to dolphins. I read books about them and their amazing abilities. Dolphins were said to have healing and telepathic abilities and a knack for opening people's hearts. I wanted to experience firsthand some of the wonders everyone wrote about.

Since I wanted to support only free dolphins, I voted with my dollars and refused the easy contacts with dolphins in captivity. I finally found dolphins in the wild in the lush waters of Hawaii.

One sunny Hawaiian day, I was swimming with two friends in a group of about seventy spinner dolphins. We forgot everything but our joy in the moment. I felt that I could swim forever with our newfound angels. And it did feel angelic. It was as though I had been lifted into heaven on earth. If there are spiritual masters on this earth, these dolphins were among them. They showed me how to feel oneness, and they took me into an envelope of safety that helped me swim and overcome my fear of deep water.

Suddenly, in the midst of our ecstasy, my friends and I each heard a loud, clear message: "Get out of the water now!"

We lifted our heads from under the water and confirmed that we had all heard the same thing. It was as if the words had been spoken out loud. Hearing the message simultaneously dazzled us; it meant that telepathy between dolphins and humans was real, not just the wishful thinking of a joyful soul.

In addition, I heard the dolphins communicate to me, "You have just enough energy to make it back to shore."

I was feeling fine and didn't see any reason for the warning. But fortunately I listened to the dolphins, because halfway to the beach my leg started to cramp. I barely arrived at the shore. As I tried to stand up, I collapsed back into the waves. The waves were small that day; otherwise, I would not have been able to crawl out of the water to shore. Obviously my angel dolphins had assessed my body's abilities, which I had totally forgotten in my ecstatic swim with them. I was oblivious to my limits, but they kept an eye on me.

How had the dolphins been able to measure my strength? How had they transmitted the message? If I had been the only one to hear the dolphins' warning, I would have considered it an act of my own intuition. But there we were, three intelligent adults, all of whom had heard the same message to get out of the water now.

Dolphins have saved many lives in the ocean. That day, when I swam with my friends and the dolphins, I understood why the ancient Greeks called them "angels of the sea."

Meditation

Have you ever been walking in the woods, swimming in the ocean, camping outdoors, or sitting quietly enjoying nature when a surprising thought or image popped into your mind? Could God have been using an animal to relay an important message about your safety, health, or well-being? Did it take courage or persistence for the animal to deliver the message?

Divine Spirit Sends in the Birds

Dorothy Weiss
Orlando, Florida

One night I awoke to a cacophony of sound. Birds were twittering, chirping, and fluttering incessantly outside our house. I was familiar with their noisy chattering at dawn, when the first rays of the sun spread gloriously across the sky and filtered through our curtained windows, creating miniature rainbows inside our house; but now the birds were calling while it was still dark. Through sleep-laden eyes, I could barely see the time on my clock radio. It was only 2:00 AM, so I tried to go back to sleep.

But what a din! The sounds did not abate. The birdcalls and shrieks built to a crescendo like a pulsating alarm. Finally I got up, thinking that I might as well watch television since I couldn't sleep anyway.

As I entered the living room, I saw a flickering yellow-orange light coming from our patio and swimming pool area. My immediate reaction was that there must be a fire. I called my husband and said, "Come quick! Something is burning outside!"

Together we ran into our backyard. There we found candles burning dangerously close to the napkins and tablecloth on our outdoor table. I had forgotten to extinguish them after serving a sentimental, old-fashioned dinner by candlelight. It hadn't become a fire yet, but a blaze could soon have started. We would have been fast asleep, practically unconscious, hearing and seeing nothing.

Alerted by the birds, we now walked through the house. We asked ourselves, "What else did we leave undone?" We discovered that the front door was unlocked, and windows in both the bathroom and kitchen had been left wide open. We usually lock the doors and close the windows at night.

After the house was secure and the candles properly snuffed out, the birds immediately fell silent.

I remember reading somewhere that Divine Spirit often gives us signals or warnings. On this night, I learned that even a sudden birdcall might be a hint to pay attention. We're glad we woke up and listened.

As far as we're concerned, the birds can sing any time they want, day or night. We welcome their serenade and all the gifts we receive from Divine Spirit every day via our animal friends.

CHAPTER NINE

Do Animals Help Us Have Strength to Survive Troubled Times?

And the glittering reins escaped out of the hands of Nestor,
And he was afraid in his heart and called out to Diomedes:
"Son of Tydeus, steer now to flight your single-foot horses."

— Homer, *The Iliad*

$\mathcal{S}$aint Francis of Assisi is known as the patron saint of animals and ecologists. Many churches conduct a ceremony called the Blessing of the Animals on his feast day of October 4. Saint Francis is often depicted surrounded by birds, which are perched on his shoulders and feeding from his hands. It was believed that he talked to the animals, giving sermons and having them listen intently to his words.

One of the most fascinating legends of Saint Francis involves his communication with a wolf. In the town of Gubbio, Italy, a wolf from the forest had begun killing cattle and people. The people in this town were in a panic and feared for their lives. They planned to destroy the wolf.

When Saint Francis arrived in Gubbio, he offered to go into the forest and meet the wolf face-to-face. But the people were afraid that Saint Francis would lose his life to the beast.

Saint Francis ignored their warnings. He walked into the forest and waited patiently for the wolf. When the animal saw this humble man, he lay down at his feet. Then Saint Francis talked to the wolf, telling the creature to stop hurting and scaring Gubbio's humans and animals. The wolf then followed Saint Francis back into town. Saint Francis told the townspeople that this was an old wolf who had lost his pack and needed food.

From that day on, the townspeople left food for the wolf, turning him into their pet. The animal never harmed anyone again. When the wolf died, the townspeople erected a monument to him in honor of the compassion and understanding that he and Brother Francis had taught them. The saint had transformed a bad situation into an opportunity for spiritual growth.

When life gets tough, have you found yourself facing the choice between being destructive and finding a more loving way to handle things? Will we have the strength, awareness, compassion, and persistence to survive troubled times?

This chapter presents answers to the questions above by recounting experiences in which animals and people assist each other in divinely guided ways during times of need or crisis. You may find their examples as inspiring as that time when a servant of God said to the hungry wolf, "Work with me on this."

The Dog Who Loved TV

Dianne Armstrong
Helena, Montana

$\mathcal{S}$adie, a little black-and-silver miniature schnauzer, was my first dog. She arrived by airplane from Spokane on a bitter cold Montana night. Sadie was so tiny that at first I couldn't see her in the crate full of shredded newspaper; I thought someone might have forgotten to send the dog. Then Sadie shook herself, stepped out of the crate, and piddled on the airport floor. This was a preview of coming attractions.

I'd always had cats before, so I didn't know anything about dogs. I just followed my heart and gave Sadie everything she wanted. Consequently, I created a monster. So we went to obedience school. Sadie didn't much take to a leash, and the choke chain definitely had to go. When on a leash, she stood stiff-legged and wouldn't move. Each time I gently tugged on the leash while saying, "heel," Sadie vomited. We got thrown out of obedience school.

Sadie loved watching TV and especially enjoyed seeing ice-skating. This sport quickly took a backseat, however, once Sadie discovered that animals appear on TV, too. She barked at everything that crawled, swam, or flew. She could even pick animals out of the cartoons.

Her favorite commercials were the Little Caesar's commercial that featured a poodle doing the bunny hop and the one that showed a toy duck floating around in a toilet bowl. Sadie would sit diligently waiting for them to appear. Her favorite show, though, besides the *Westminster Dog Show,* was *Northern Exposure.* As soon as the music started, Sadie charged to the set, trembling with anticipation and waiting for the moose to stroll across the screen. When the moose appeared, Sadie went ballistic. It was hilarious.

At age five, Sadie suffered stroke-like symptoms and almost died. My husband and I took turns sitting with her around the clock, day after day. Eventually she improved, but she lost the vision in her left eye and some use of her left limbs. She was no longer able to take long walks with us, but she howled when we left her behind so we found a baby backpack to be the perfect solution. Sadie loved it when we carried her on walks in it.

Dianne's Sadie

Sadie accompanied me through the best and worst years of my life: getting sober, changing jobs, the deaths of two grandparents, getting married (Sadie even came to our formal wedding reception), moving, and — the toughest chapter of all — losing my only brother, Larry, to AIDS. Six months after Larry died in my arms, Sadie also slipped away, at the age of eight.

When Sadie died, I didn't think I could bear it. The night of her passing, I knelt by our bed and begged God for a sign — just this once — to let me know that Sadie was warm and happy (she hated being cold). I needed to know that Sadie was okay.

Immediately after I spoke this prayer, the northern lights (which

I had never seen before) suddenly appeared outside our window with a brilliance of color beyond description. My husband and I never found anyone else in our area who saw this ten-minute display, and it wasn't reported in our local newspaper the next day. No *Northern Exposure* theme song played, but I knew that these northern lights were the perfect answer to my prayer about Sadie.

We also have a peace lily that has hung in our bedroom for years, near where Sadie always slept. Although the lily had never bloomed and or even had a bud, on the morning after Sadie's death we awoke to find a beautiful bloom. The lily bloomed again on the first anniversary of Sadie's death and also the second. For six years so far, Sadie's plant has continued to bloom once a year and only on special days, such as the anniversary of the date we started Montana Pets on the Net, a webpage to help rescue animals in need.

Recently our other mini-schnauzer, Rosie, also passed away. The night Rosie died, I asked Sadie to please send me a bloom on her plant to let me know when Rosie found her. The plant had already bloomed the previous month on Valentine's Day, so imagine our surprise when a big bud appeared three days after I made my request to Sadie and then was joined by another bloom! It brings me great joy to know that Rosie is now reunited forever with her favorite tug-partner, Sadie.

Meditation

Was an animal there to help when you were faced with what seemed like insurmountable challenges? In what ways have animals made you smile through your tears?

Our Angel Kitty

Donna Moody
Oakville, Connecticut

Many times we wake up and feel as if the world is spinning out of control. It's then that our animal friends make us feel relaxed, happy, and better able to cope with life. Our kitty, Vito, is a cat who knew how to be an angel and lessen the burdens of a special-needs dog.

Several years ago, our neighbors inherited a chocolate-colored poodle named Willie. Since they weren't able to care for the dog full-time, Willie lived with us part-time. This arrangement worked out very well. Willie loved to play ball, take walks, and go for rides. He was an excellent pet for all of us.

Then our neighbor passed away, and Willie came to live with us. By then, the dog was blind and deaf but still happy.

One day, the sun shone through an angel ornament that was hanging in our kitchen window. I looked out through the ray of sunlight and saw a little orange-and-white kitty sitting on an old tire in the backyard. He had been placed there as a gift by a priest friend of ours, Father Vito. When we adopted the kitty, we named him Vito.

As Vito became friends with Willie, he would walk alongside the blind dog to guide and protect him from danger. We called Vito the seeing-eye kitty. Vito would also sit at the edge of the yard to block the way so that Willie couldn't wander into the street. If Vito thought Willie was outside alone, he would beg to go out and be near him.

I truly believe that Vito is a guardian angel sent from heaven to protect our handicapped dog. There are no words to describe the special bond that exists between Vito and Willie and the closeness they share.

Donna's Vito

Meditation

Have you noticed animals showing extraordinary compassion to each other through troubled times? Is there a divine hand guiding them to give without expecting anything in return?

The Luck Bunny

Camille A. Lufkin
Fort Edward, New York

I won a rabbit in a raffle. Please don't ask me why I entered the raffle. I had sworn not to come home with another rabbit. I already had two: my loyal and loving Gekko, and my mischievous and flighty Flippity. The minute I stood in front of the raffled rabbit's cage, a sinking feeling came over me. As I sulked off to have my lunch, I wondered, "What have I done?"

But as I was eating and grumbling, a feeling of calm suddenly came over me. I took a deep breath and relaxed. Somehow I knew that everything would be all right. If I was meant to have this rabbit, things would work out.

The rabbit, a seal-point Netherlands Dwarf, was tiny, weighing only two pounds at two years old. She fit perfectly in my hand. Her dark eyes were huge, but she had tiny ears. I quickly fell in love and called her my little luck bunny. She was the mother of grand champions, and now she was mine.

Her registered name was Diamond Girl, but this seemed too long for such a little rabbit. I began calling her my little Gem. She carried herself with as much dignity as a Victorian lady, but she also had it in her nature to punch the cat on the nose and teach her to respect bunnies.

Over the next few months, Gem went through many ordeals.

She fought off the beginning stages of uterine cancer and had to have emergency surgery. Even through that battle, she had enough spunk to spit out her medicines, punch, grumble, and growl. She'd always end each medication session, though, by snuggling and licking my hand. She spent hours on my lap, nudging me for pettings. This little bunny had tons of spirit and lots of love.

One day, I remembered that calm feeling I'd had when I first met Gem. After overcoming so many health challenges, she seemed destined for more than just being my pet. As docile and loving as she was, I sensed that Gem had a greater purpose.

I had read about pets doing service as therapy animals in hospitals and nursing homes. It began to occur to me that Gem would be perfect for this kind of work. A friend told me that a volunteer group in our area brought a variety of animals to local nursing homes, including dogs, cats,

Camille's Gem

rabbits, and even a llama. I called the representative of this organization and volunteered to take Gem for a visit.

Gem was a natural. Sitting up in her basket, wearing a tiny leash and harness, she watched everything with her big eyes. Her little ears perked straight up. Staff and guests hurried over to see the rabbit. They asked if she was real or a stuffed toy, because she was so quiet and calm. Gem basked in the attention and sat up on her hind legs for a better view.

When we went to visit the residents that first night, Gem won the hearts of everyone she met. One man's face lit up when he saw her. He told me about rabbits he'd had as a child. Later, one of the staff said that this gentleman rarely spoke and almost never smiled.

A blind woman patted Gem with her arthritic hands and cooed to her. The emotions emanating from these people were some of the strongest and most honest I'd ever felt. Watching their faces as they held and loved my little rabbit was like seeing a miracle unfold in front of me. Through it all, Gem sat quietly, nudging people's hands with her nose and occasionally giving someone a quick lick with her tongue. Once she even sat up and washed her face — a true sign of how happy and content she was to be among all these loving people.

As we packed up to leave, one woman caught my hand, her eyes brimming with tears. She said, "Please, you will bring her back again, won't you?"

I knew then that this was why I had won the little luck bunny. Her purpose in life was to bring love to many more people than me and to soothe and heal them. I had been chosen to bring her where she was most needed. She truly was a Gem among rabbits.

Meditation

Who have been the "gem" animals in your life? Were there diamonds in the rough — people or animals — who at first didn't look as if they'd be healing agents, but became exactly what you or someone else needed?

Support through a Team Effort

Nancy Harlett
Tiffin, Ohio

*F*red and Charity were truly an odd couple. Fred was a little dog of undetermined breed. I've often theorized that his momma was a terrier and his daddy was a traveling salesman. Fred entered my world when he wandered up to a beach where I was on lifeguard duty. He was all ribs and fleas and obviously starved, but he ignored kids' offers of food. He walked right over to me, lay down beside me, and heaved a big sigh as if he were home at last. And so he was. I took Fred home with me that day.

Later that year, a woman stopped her car in front of my sister-in-law's house, pulled a tiny gray kitten out of her car's fan belt, threw the baby behind some bushes, and drove away. I took the kitten home, nursed the tiny creature back to health, and named her Charity.

During this time, I was trying to breed and raise Siamese cats to help pay for all the animal rescue work I do. Often the mother cats didn't have enough milk to feed their babies because there were too many of them. At other times, the mother would reject a kitten for some unknown reason. But Charity, through sheer maternal instinct, was able to wish milk into her body and take over nursing the rejected kittens. She and Fred became a team: Charity nursed the kitties, and Fred helped wash them. He usually licked them backward, so they had spiked hairdos, but this didn't matter. Fred's licking gave them the stimulation that new kittens need to keep their digestive systems functioning.

Nancy's Charity and her kitten

As time went on, Fred and Charity saved at least a dozen kittens each year through their teamwork of nursing and licking, and both of them lived to a ripe old age. Fred was nearly eighteen years old when his strokes forced the final trip to the vet. Charity was close to nineteen years old when breast cancer took her from us. These two kind creatures remained the best of friends, and even death did not part them. We buried them together in my backyard under an enormous French lilac bush. Each spring, the bush has over five hundred blossoms of long, pale, lavender blooms.

Meditation

Have animals ever teamed up to help you or others survive? What do their examples teach about the power of pulling together?

A Squirrel Reminded Us to Trust God

Allen and Linda Anderson
Minneapolis, Minnesota

*O*ne day years ago we decided, like so many people in this era of entrepreneurship, to start a homegrown project. We planned to share stories about the spiritual connection between people and animals. Our dream was to inspire people around the world through animals who were spiritual catalysts in the lives of humans. We coined a slogan to describe our efforts: Increasing Love and Respect for All Life — One Story at a Time.

We had many experiences of our own, but we wanted to find out if other people had stories of spiritual experiences with animals. We put up flyers in coffee shops, placed notices on internet chat groups, and asked friends and strangers a question: Are animals teaching you spiritual lessons? Within a few weeks, we were inundated with hundreds of stories from many countries. We decided to publish our first *Angel Animals Newsletter* to present these stories about the powerful, but largely unacknowledged, spiritual bond between humans and animals. We eventually received so many stories that we decided to turn this stimulating project into a full-blown adventure. We intended to write books, facilitate workshops, and establish a website to reach as many people as possible with these stories and their uplifting messages.

After asking for divine guidance, we believed that Spirit was lighting a path for us to follow with this project. We forged ahead, taking to heart the adage about doing what you love. That's when we did what the wise financial advisors say not to do: we both left our day jobs and devoted ourselves full-time to establishing the Angel Animals Network. We were soon to discover that the pursuit of big dreams requires even bigger efforts than we'd ever imagined.

We launched the Angel Animals Network with friends and family cheering us on. We plunged in, giving most of our attention and resources to the project, working long hours, and investing our savings. We were giddy with excitement at the slightest hints of success, baying our songs of delight to the moon.

Then, as the pursuit of dreams often goes, the work grew harder and the rewards fewer. Everything cost more, took longer, and was more difficult than we thought it would be. Before long, our goals seemed distant and unattainable.

We asked each other and God, "Did we make the right decision to pursue such grand and impossible goals?" When we asked for guidance in the beginning, had we misunderstood the direction God had indicated?

One day, we hit our lowest point. We were bone-weary of trying to figure out how to make things work according to our plans. We decided to chill out by taking a nap upstairs, and we each fell into a deep sleep. When we went back downstairs, we found an unexpected visitor in the living room.

Our cat Cuddles, only a few months old at the time, was standing on her hind legs, batting toward something that was making a lot of noise behind the television cabinet in the corner. Our dog, Taylor, ran in circles. When Allen looked in the corner, he found a squirrel who was taller than Cuddles. He immediately scooped up the kitten and put her and Taylor in another room.

How had a squirrel gotten into our living room? The fireplace's glass door was closed. No wild animal had ever come into our house. The squirrel's appearance was a mystery. We decided to coax the frightened animal out of his hiding place and steer him toward the living room door.

But the wind howled ominously outside; it was a cold, dark Minnesota winter night. Each time we got the squirrel to sprint from behind the cabinet, he found a way to avoid the open door and return to his hiding place. After several tries, we finally figured out all his escape routes. One by one, we sealed them off by putting up makeshift barriers.

As Linda talked to the squirrel, reassuring him that everything would be all right, we began listening to her words. She was saying, "Trust us. We're only closing off the ways that keep you trapped inside. It looks scary, but you'll be free if you just go through that door."

We looked at each other in amazement as we began to understand the message that was meant for us, not just for the squirrel. Our fears of not fulfilling our goals had made us incapable of hearing anything but the pounding of our frightened hearts. Now a little squirrel had been sent to teach us to trust and surrender to God's bigger and better plan. That night, we were being shown the truth: what we'd viewed as obstacles had all along been God's way of preventing us from going the wrong ways.

At last, we were able to steer the squirrel to the open door. His face seemed to reflect a dawning awareness that plunging into the darkness was his only choice. He stood in the doorway for a minute, turned, and looked at us. Then he bowed his little head, as if to say good-bye, and hurtled into the wind.

After our visitor left, we sat down on the sofa, exhausted and humbled. We hugged each other. In our fear, we hadn't considered the possibility that God might be pushing us into a corner because that's where we'd find the doorway to freedom. With a squirrel's help, we could now recognize that we were being guided in the best and wisest ways. We said sincerely to God, "Thy will be done." By surrendering and trusting, as our squirrel messenger had done, we began to relax, listen, and enjoy the journey.

Our trust was rewarded. Our first book became a bestseller, and our work has been featured in wire-service articles and on national television. But more important, we were able to reach millions of people with stories of animals whose divinely directed actions deliver the message that love, blessings, and miracles are all around.

Kahlil Gibran wrote: "When you work, you are a flute through whose heart the whispering of the hours turns to music."[1] Pure and loving hearts become flutes that the Divine plays to uplift all life.

PART FOUR

COMFORT

*When a sage is present and you sit near him
or her, you feel peace and light.*

— Thich Nhat Hanh

CHAPTER TEN

Do Dreams of Animals Contain Spiritual Messages?

I would fly to the woods' low rustle
And the meadows' kindly page.
Let me dream as of old by the river,
And be loved for the dream always;
For a dreamer lives forever,
And a toiler dies in a day.

— John Boyle O'Reilly, "The Cry of a Dreamer"

*D*reaming serves to make us healthier — mentally, physically, and emotionally. But do dreams improve our spiritual health as well?

A 1995 cover story in *Life* magazine, "The Power of Dreams," recounted some dreams of famous people. Journalist George Howe Colt wrote, "Dreams have been credited with the creation of Mont St. Michel, the discovery of the structure of the benzene molecule, fixing Jack Nicklaus's golf swing, Lyndon Johnson's decision not to run for reelection in 1968, many of the routes mapped out by Harriet Tubman for the Underground Railroad, and enough novels, poems, and paintings to fill the libraries and museums of a small civilization."[1]

Over the years, we've received many stories from people who had animals appear to them in dreams to alert them to problems, tell them where to find a lost pet, or say a final good-bye after death. Are dreams one more way in which God works through animal messengers to let us know that a divine and loving hand guides our lives?

In this chapter, you will meet a variety of individuals whose dreams involving animals are nothing short of miraculous.

I Dreamed of DeeDee

Sharon Ward
Raleigh, North Carolina

My cat, Alpha, came to live with me when she was six weeks old. She is a beautiful black tabby with big gold eyes. Over the past eleven years, we have grown to love each other very much. She's like my own child.

Several years ago, I thought I might lose Alpha. She and I had moved into an apartment with a new roommate who was "cat-less." This was the first time Alpha had ever experienced being the only cat in the family.

I worked full-time, but I lived close enough to come home for lunch. Alpha's usual behavior, before we moved, was to run up to me when I came in the door. In our new apartment, I wasn't as welcome; Alpha had developed an allergy, and my noon visits entailed applying some awful medicine and giving Alpha a bath to help heal her skin. It was torture for both of us when I applied the medicine.

I noticed that Alpha was becoming increasingly depressed and lonely. She spent most of the time sleeping in her cat box. She no longer greeted me. I was distraught. I feared that Alpha's emotional state wasn't helping her to heal.

This condition went on for a couple of months. I was very busy at work, and I had volunteer duties in the evenings and on weekends. I hardly had a moment to think about what to do for my dear

Alpha, who seemed to be slowly slipping away from me. I desperately asked God for help.

Then one night I had a dream. In the dream, I saw Alpha nursing a large kitten — a multicolored tabby with jelly-roll striping. The weird thing about this kitten was that she was really too old to be nursed. When I awoke from the dream, I told my roommate about it. We agreed that God had answered my question in this dream: I should get Alpha a companion so that she wouldn't be lonely.

With my heavy work schedule, I didn't know how I would find a kitten for Alpha. Besides, it was about a week before Thanksgiving. I had plans to fly to Wisconsin to visit my family for a week.

Sharon's DeeDee and Alpha

I believed that I had to find a kitten before I left on the trip. That way, I reasoned, Alpha wouldn't feel I had abandoned her. On Saturday afternoon of the weekend when I was to leave, I finished up loose ends at my office and began to skim through the day's newspaper for ads about free kittens. There were only two ads for kittens, and just one of the phone numbers was in my area. When I called, I learned that one kitten from the litter was left.

I hurried to the house and agreed to take home an eight-week-old female striped tabby. I quickly whisked her up and placed her in a box for the short ride home. When I took her out of the box, I realized that she looked exactly like the kitten with jelly-roll striping I had seen in my dream.

Of course, Alpha wasn't happy to see this stranger in her house. She hissed and spit at the new arrival. I wondered if I'd made a big mistake. I worried that Alpha would hate me for this further indignity after what she'd endured with my attempts to heal her allergy. But there was nothing I could do now because I was leaving for Wisconsin the next morning. My roommate said she'd look after the kitties while I was gone. I spent the entire vacation worrying about what I'd find when I returned.

I came home to a surprising sight. Alpha and the new kitten, DeeDee, had become very close while I was gone — so close that DeeDee would suckle on Alpha, just as she had been doing in my dream.

Soon Alpha was fully healed from her allergies and depression. She and DeeDee became the best of companions. These cats and my dream serve as reminders of the depth of God's love for all life.

Meditation

Have you had a prophetic dream involving an animal? Was there some kind of guidance or instruction in the dream that enabled you to better care for yourself or an animal?

Dreaming of My Animal Spirit

Hope Catherine Ball, MEd
Lake Monroe, Florida

One day I answered a newspaper ad about a white shepherd dog named Dakota who needed a home. Dakota had been abused and was considered too mentally disturbed to be sent to a pound. I was asked to have an interview with someone from the Connecticut Friends of Animals before I adopted her. I cancelled all my plans for the day and drove to Hartford to meet Dakota. All I could think about was how this poor dog was alone in the world, and I wanted to be there for her.

I showed up at the small apartment of Brandy, a nice woman from the Connecticut Friends of Animals. She showed me where to find Dakota hiding behind a dresser in the bedroom. Brandy's apartment was full of animals, but none of them were as frightened as Dakota. She told me that Dakota had been beaten and left for dead in her former owner's backyard. She had gone without food or water for days. She had whittled her bottom teeth down to the gums in an attempt to chew the chain that held her. The animal rescue team spent many hours getting Dakota out of her doghouse.

I immediately fell in love with Dakota. After Brandy interviewed me, I was approved to adopt her. When it was time to leave, I spent quite a while convincing Dakota to get into the car. I finally had to lift her up and place her in the front seat. She was so scared that she shook all the way to my home in New London. Along the way, I stopped at the store and bought her food and a bed. When we got into my house, she had an accident on the floor. I just hugged and petted her for hours. Even my cats felt at ease with this timid, gentle dog.

The next day, I took Dakota to work with me. She sat under my desk, and no one even knew she was there. That night, I taught her to chew on a dog bone because she didn't know how. I lay down beside her and pretended to chew on one end while she gnawed on the other.

Dakota and I were inseparable. I took her everywhere, and I noticed that she was very intuitive. She was always mystical, bright, and aware. In the years we spent together, she only barked once — and that was when a neighbor entered my house without knocking. She seemed to watch people all the time. She was so silent that she could enter a room and, unless you looked right at her, you wouldn't know she was there.

Hope's Dakota

Dakota could also sense danger. One day I was packing up my things for a trip to the beach. As Dakota watched me preparing to leave, she would not stop pawing at me or at the door. She was acting very weird. She followed me around the house, whining and pacing until I took her outside. Then she refused to go back inside. Finally I decided to bring her with me to the beach. When we returned, my house was surrounded by fire trucks and police cars. It had burned down! I believe Dakota knew something was about to happen and was trying to tell me to leave but not without her!

Because Dakota was so mystical and soothing, I grew to always want her near me. She was my best friend. She did so much for me over the years. My heart broke when Dakota died, but death has not separated us; Dakota continues to help me from the other side.

Soon after Dakota died, I got a letter telling me that the lease was up on the house where I lived. I had the choice of either paying more for rent each month or moving. I was already paying as much as I could handle, so I needed to find another rental right away. Because I had eight animals, it was hard for me to find an affordable place.

At the time, I had been studying with a wise woman named Jae, who suggested that a shaman named Maggie might be able to help me. Maggie and I drummed together, and we went into a meditative trance to find my animal spirit. While in the trance, we arrived at a place where Dakota was the only animal spirit. No other animal spirits came to us. I told Dakota that I needed a place to live, and she said that she could help. Dakota told me to look where she looks, and I would see the place. Then she told me to close my eyes, and that when I opened them again I would be able to see what she sees.

Maggie waited patiently while I looked through Dakota's eyes (she was comically short) and saw a place in the country with gray tiles on the wall. All I saw were tiles; that was the image Dakota gave me. But I understood what to do; I must find this place with gray tiles at knee level (Dakota's height) and rent it.

The next day, I called a realtor. She told me about a place in the country that was for rent. I was thrilled, and went to see it that week. The house was great, but there wasn't a tile in sight. In spite of this,

I decided to rent it. The place was badly in need of cleaning, so I arranged to clean it up as payment for the first month's rent.

After I moved in, I was under the kitchen sink one day cleaning out copious amounts of garbage. That's when I found a large gray tile. I turned over the tile and saw the name "Dakota" handwritten in blue letters on the back of it. I knew I had found the place Dakota was trying to guide me to; I was home.

I still see Dakota in my dreams. In fact, one day I was feeling scared about my future. I thought my job situation would never improve. Dakota came to me in a dream that night and told me to wait until morning before thinking about this situation again. The next morning, I awoke to the telephone ringing. It was someone from the university calling to say they needed an instructor; I was hired over the phone.

Long ago, I saved Dakota's life. She had been beaten, abused, and left for dead. I guess she never forgot the favor, because now she saves me every day.

An Iguana's Nightmare

Darry Conner
Durham, North Carolina

Iguanas are inexpensive to adopt as pets, but they are complicated and expensive to care for properly. Over 1 million baby iguanas are imported annually, and 90 percent never make it through their first year. Pet stores don't usually give accurate information on how to raise them. That cute little baby iguana, who starts out weighing less than an ounce, will grow to over twenty pounds and be eighteen to twenty inches long from its nose to the base of its tail — and five to seven feet long including the tail. Properly cared for, an iguana can live as long as twenty years in captivity. But that cuddly little lizard has to be carefully tamed to live in a human home.

The rescue group I belong to discourages people from adopting iguanas unless they read *Iguanas for Dummies*[2] and know exactly what challenges they'll be facing. We ask prospective adopters to see and hold an adult iguana to find out if they will be comfortable with a BIG lizard.

Obviously, I have done my homework on what it takes to care for iguanas — things such as the need for fresh, hand-washed, chopped produce every day; perfect temperature modulation and high humidity so that they can thermoregulate; and the need to keep their areas clean and disinfected to prevent salmonella, which they can carry. I thought I had taken every precaution to protect our new baby iguana, Bubbette. But one night I dreamed that Bubbette somehow got into the churning garbage disposal in our kitchen and was killed. I woke up in the middle of the night crying loudly from that horrible nightmare.

Darry's Bubbette

Several months later, long after I'd forgotten the dream, Bubbette was sitting on my shoulder in the kitchen as I moved around cleaning up the dishes. I pushed scraps down the garbage disposal and switched it on. When I turned around to pick up more dishes, I had a flashback of that dream. Immediately, I spun back to the sink and flicked off the disposal — just in time. Bubbette, for the first time ever, had taken a flying leap off my shoulder into the sink. I caught her just as she was going down the disposal drain.

If I had not remembered that dream, Bubbette probably would have fallen into the garbage disposal before I could realize what was happening. She was very small at the time, and would have slid easily into the hole and met an untimely demise. Needless to say, from that day on I declined my iguana's invitations to help me out in the kitchen.

Meditation

What if the messages in dreams aren't merely workings of our subconscious minds or the result of what we ate before bedtime? Has an animal communicated with you in a dream about a matter of great importance?

The Doggie Dream Diagnosis

Richard S. McDiarmid
Langley, British Columbia

*D*uring the 1980s, I worked for an engineering and manufacturing company where I was responsible for managing research and development. Three or four times a year, I was required to travel to Japan as a technical support representative. This often involved two-week intervals of intense meetings and travel throughout the Japanese islands.

On one such trip, I had completed a long day of work and was thankful to go to my bed in a small inn. I had just fallen asleep when I was "awakened" in a dream by my seventeen-year-old dog, Sinbad, licking my face. He expressed his love and joy and seemed very excited to see me. As I responded to this outpouring of love, I looked down to see a dark hole or void in Sinbad's chest. Something was wrong with this picture. I felt as if I were looking into deep space without starlight. Startled, I awakened to find that, of course, I was thousands of miles from home. My dog was far away and not physically by my side.

Had something happened at home? I wondered if I should call, but I decided it would not be wise. I might upset my wife and family and concern them needlessly about Sinbad.

The week's work played out, and I returned home to find that all was well. Sinbad greeted me happily at the door.

A few days after my return, I sat in my easy chair and reached down to pet Sinbad. As I stroked him, I became aware of a big lump on his chest in the very spot where I had observed the dark hole in my dream. We took Sinbad to our veterinarian, who took X-rays and concluded that our dog had a large tumor. He was operated on and survived, living another two years.

I have always been grateful for Sinbad's appearance in my dream, when he let me know what he needed to continue living and bringing love and joy to our home.

Richard's Sinbad

Meditation

Has an animal ever appeared in your dreams to tell you what he or she needed? Did you follow the advice? What happened?

The Cat Who Guided My Dad Home

Leslie-Ann Guiney
Scarborough, Ontario

$\mathcal{I}$ adopted Billy from the Toronto Humane Society. He was a scruffy, orange, wormy kitten with a terrible upper-respiratory infection. I knew his rehabilitation would cost a lot of money, but when this kitten looked at me we both knew in an instant that he was for me and I was for him. I named him "Billy" after King William of Orange, the king that most Northern Irish people revere. Because of this, my father — who had immigrated to Canada from Belfast — loved Billy more than any of my other cats.

Billy loved everyone. He would lie on the floor and wait to be touched. But he especially loved my dad. Whenever Dad came for a visit, Billy ran straight to him. My father had a terrible heart condition, and Billy had always been sickly, so these two creatures with their poor health in common became fast friends.

Later, I adopted a cat named Merlin without knowing that he had feline infectious peritonitis (FIP). That virus soon killed him and, two weeks later, took Billy's life. I was devastated by the loss of my two boy cats, but Billy's death had a significant impact on Dad. Only a few months later, my father's heart condition worsened to the point where he had to be scheduled for his second bypass operation. He was given a 70/30 chance of making it, and we were excited at the thought that the operation might give him a new lease on life.

Dad had his surgery in the morning, and we saw him that afternoon. He was pretty much out it from the drugs he had been given, but he was able to tell us via sign language that a cat had been with him during his surgery. We didn't know which cat he was talking about, and we thought he might be hallucinating from the drugs. We left Dad at the hospital that night and went home to get a much-needed night's sleep.

That night I dreamed of Billy. In my dream, he was perfectly formed and vibrantly colored. I woke up crying from the warm feeling of seeing my dear friend again. I remember telling Billy how happy I was to have him back and that I was honored that he'd chosen to return to me. What I didn't realize was that Billy was trying to tell me something in this dream.

When my mother and I went back to the hospital to see Dad the next day, there he was, sitting up, right as rain, and writing messages on a clipboard because he was still intubated and couldn't talk. He told us that he loved us, and that he felt better than he had in a long time. He said he was going to get out of the hospital and go home. He offered to help me wallpaper my bedroom when he was well enough. We were ecstatic at his remarkable progress.

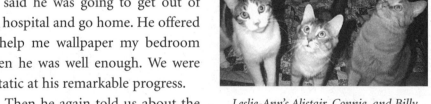

Leslie-Ann's Alistair, Connie, and Billy

Then he again told us about the cat, whom he now identified as Billy, who had been with him during surgery. He said he had felt Billy jump on the bed, walk to his hand and rub his head on it, then flop over. Mom and I looked at each other and laughed, because that is exactly what Billy would have done. The visit was cut short by the arrival of the respiratory therapist, who came in to check on Dad's breathing. I had to leave his room before I could tell Dad about my own dream of Billy.

We sat in the waiting room for forty-five minutes. Then a nurse appeared and told us that we should call anyone who needed to say good-bye to Dad, since they didn't think he would make it through the night. My mother was shocked by this news and broke down in tears. I felt a bit more prepared because by then I had made the connection between Billy's appearance in my dream and the fact that my father's death was near. Because of this dream, I was calmer and better able to console my mother. Ten minutes later, the nurse returned to say that they had done all they could, but were very sorry; Dad had passed away.

That was when the significance of my dream and Dad's words about Billy made sense. Billy had come in the dream to tell me that everything would be okay — that he was going to be with Dad to guide him, if you will.

Is it a coincidence that this kitten, who had a respiratory problem, helped to guide a human who died of respiratory failure? Is it a mere coincidence that this sick little kitten died only three months prior to my father's death?

I know that Billy was here for a reason; he came to guide Dad home. I truly believe that animals are here for us, and that we're here for them. They should be respected and recognized for the hefty spiritual burdens they carry without ever asking for anything in return.

White Horse Dream

Laurence Cruz
Los Angeles, California

*H*orses have appeared many times in my dreams over the years, often representing the raw, unconditional power and beauty of Divine Spirit in my life.

One such dream was particularly symbolic and memorable. The setting was a land of mountains and lakes, and serene flute and piano music played throughout. The entire dream was in slow motion, accentuating the sense of grace.

In the distance, galloping along a path toward me, came a white horse. On its back, dressed all in white, was a jockey wearing a white shirt and pants, a white cap, white boots, and white gloves.

This graceful, harmonious unit of man and horse drew slowly closer to me until it passed within feet of where I stood. As it did, I noticed a key detail: Instead of pushing his charge to go faster by beating him with a whip, the rider gently caressed the horse's neck with his gloved hand.

This brief dream vision spoke volumes to me about spiritual mastery and the relationship between the true self, the soul, and the human self. I understood it to mean that the human self (the jockey) never needs to struggle or use force in order to realize all of its true goals. Rather, the self needs to harness the power of soul (the horse) and simply allow it to have its way. This is achieved by trusting that

the human and divine selves, far from being in conflict, have perfectly mutual interests. Struggle comes from the lack of that trust,
and from the resulting pursuit of goals that are not in keeping with
our true nature.

Like a Thoroughbred racehorse, the soul needs little, if any, training. It simply needs to be harnessed and to have obstacles removed
from its path. It will do the rest, if we allow it.

Animals are showing many people that the spiritual harmony between the dream state and their waking lives elevates dreaming to a
new level of importance.

CHAPTER ELEVEN

Do Animals Go Peacefully into the Light?

Farewell, dear voyageur, 'twill not be long.
Your work is done, now may peace rest with thee.
Your kindly thoughts and deeds, they will live on.
This is not death, 'tis immortality.

— Unknown, "There Is No Death"

nimal messengers have much to teach us about death, the dying process, heaven, and God's eternal love for all souls. Many people have had mystical encounters after animals have passed over to the other side. These experiences offer glimmers of hope, peace, and enlightenment about the afterlife.

Reverend Andrew Linzey, an Anglican priest who holds the post of animal theologian at Mansfield College at Oxford, says, "I have no doubt that animals will have an afterlife. The question isn't whether they will be there in heaven, since they are sinless and innocent. The real question is whether humans, who are violent, sinful, and faithless, will be there."[1] Does animal consciousness survive death? Is it possible that animals communicate from the heavenly realms with grieving people they have left behind?

As you'll see in this chapter's stories, many people have had after-death contact with animal companions. People often say that, at the moment of death, they saw a flash of light or an ethereal spirit leap from an animal's dying body. When our cat Mugsie died, Linda was holding him in her arms. She saw the cat's light-body fly out of its twenty-one-year-old physical body. The spirit of Mugsie looked as healthy and playful as a kitten and seemed happy to shed his decayed and sickly shell.

Do animals fear death? Unwanted animals who are about to be euthanized, slaughtered inhumanely, or hunted down often fight to stay alive.[2] Conversely, we've been amazed at how many animals compassionately let their humans know that it is okay to release them when the time is right.

Whether an animal has had to be relieved of pain and suffering or died at a ripe old age, people who have lost their animal friends need comfort and understanding. Over the years, many have found solace by reading an anonymously written piece called "The Rainbow Bridge."

The Rainbow Bridge

Anonymous

Just this side of Heaven is a place called the Rainbow Bridge. When an animal dies who has been especially close to someone here, that pet goes to the Rainbow Bridge. There are meadows and hills for all of our special friends so they can run and play together. There is plenty of food and water and sunshine, and our friends are warm and comfortable. All the animals who had been ill and old are restored to health and vigor; those who were hurt or maimed are made whole and strong again, just as we remember them in our dreams of days and times gone by.

The animals are happy and content, except for one small thing: They miss someone very special to them who had to be left behind.

They all run and play together, but the day comes when one suddenly stops and looks into the distance. The bright eyes are intent; the eager body quivers. Suddenly he begins to break away from the group, flying over the green grass, his legs carrying him faster and faster. YOU have been spotted, and when you and your special friend finally meet, you cling together in joyous reunion, never to be parted again. The happy kisses rain upon your face; your hands again caress the beloved head, and you look once more into the trusting eyes of your pet, so long gone from your life but never absent from your heart.

Then you cross the Rainbow Bridge together...

Messengers from Heaven

Judy Neely
Missoula, Montana

My American Kennel Club (AKC)–registered Boston terrier, Molly, was a messenger from heaven. That is the best way to describe her presence on earth and how she touched my life and the lives of many others. To this day, Molly still touches others with her love and with God's love that flows through her.

Molly and I could communicate with a glance or through our thoughts. She seemed always to know what I was thinking, and she reacted almost before I said anything to her. We were connected spiritually both on earth and after death. I also know that God had a mission for Molly, and she fulfilled it.

When I was the director of an Alzheimer's unit, I took Molly to work with me every day. She became the guardian angel of the unit. She touched hundreds of lives. She gave people their last smiles. She lay on the beds of the dying so they wouldn't die alone. Anyone could look into Molly's eyes and see that she loved God.

Molly seemed to know exactly what to do with the patients. She became their dogs of long ago. They called her Spot, Rex, Fritz, Puppy, or Blackie, and she answered to all those names. She comforted those who sat and cried softly, licking the tears off their faces. She did silly things that made them laugh. She walked with them. She gladly cleaned up the vegetables or other food they dropped on the floor at mealtime. She watched over patients who were getting up out of wheelchairs and weren't supposed to be walking. She guarded the unit from strangers.

After several years in the Alzheimer's unit, we began to work with Home Health, visiting private homes, nursing homes, and assisted-living care centers. Molly was welcomed into every home. The Delta Society, an organization that offers training and certification for service and therapy dogs, gave Molly an honorary award for being a Certified Therapy Dog and Canine Good Citizen.

I was amazed at how much Molly gave to others, but I was even more astonished by what she gave to me. She showed courage, bravery, a sweet spirit, patience, and gentleness. Sometimes I would sit on the floor and ask her who she really was and what she was supposed to teach me.

Judy's Molly

Two days before Molly went to the Rainbow Bridge, she was sleeping on her beanbag in the living room beside the large sliding-glass door. I did not know then that she would be gone so soon. I looked out the glass door and saw a beautiful rainbow had formed over the house. Molly on her beanbag was in the center of the rainbow. It was especially odd that a rainbow appeared, because it wasn't raining. The rainbow reminded me of the Rainbow Bridge and the fact that Molly would be there to greet me someday.

After Molly made her journey to the Rainbow Bridge, I learned some of what she was meant to teach, for she didn't leave alone. She took part of me with her, because we shared a heartbeat.

A week after Molly passed over, I sat in my den reading "The Rainbow Bridge." I was thinking that someone had made this up to make people feel better. I was writhing, fighting, and dying inside over the loss of Molly. I asked God if there really is a Rainbow Bridge.

At that moment, exactly one week to the hour after Molly crossed over, the biggest, brightest rainbow appeared over my house — again framing the beanbag where Molly used to sleep. My tears flowed. It was as if Molly were saying, "Here I am, Mom. I'm fine." And God was saying, "I have her, Judy. She is fine. My promise to you is that, yes, there is a Rainbow Bridge."

Since her journey back to God, Molly continues to give me "hello"s from heaven to let me know that she's very much around. Molly also sends messages to friends of mine who were close to her.

Rainbows appeared again on my first birthday after Molly crossed over, and for two years in a row on Molly's birthday. I believe that rainbows honor and mark the passage of her life — a life that was both divine and spiritual. Time and time again, on special dates, these rainbows come, convincing me that Molly, God, and I are all connected.

Bitsy Says Good-Bye

Heidi W. Dunlap
Houston, Texas

For twelve years, my parents were the proud companions of a little red long-haired dachshund by the name of Bitsy. Most of us have had special pets in our lives, and many can point to one or two animals who had something extra-special, whether in intelligence, emotional qualities, or personality. Bitsy had an unusual intelligence, and she kept my parents laughing most of her life with her antics. She was also a beloved traveling companion, and they rarely went anywhere without her.

Each morning on his way to work, my father would take Bitsy to spend the day with my grandmother. He would say to Bitsy, "Are you ready to go see Memaw?" Her ears would perk up. She would race to the door and then jump in the car. Once she was at my grandmother's house, Bitsy would demand her treat and proceed to ignore everyone until she'd finished enjoying it. My grandmother called her "granddog," and doted on Bitsy as if she were her own beloved pet.

Recently my grandmother had had to move into an assisted-living home that was out of town. My father wasn't able to take Bitsy to spend the day with Grandmother in her new place. Only on rare occasions could Grandmother see her granddog, and both of them missed their visits. In late September and October, Grandmother had several severe setbacks that left us believing she might go at any moment. During her less lucid moments she was heard speaking to someone, as if her deceased husband or father might have been standing next to her.

At last, Grandmother began a slow process of recovery. After she was well enough, we moved her into a nursing home five miles from my parents' house. This allowed the family to be with her more often. By this time, Bitsy was twelve years old and had developed a bad heart murmur. At times she became terribly short of breath, so she wasn't in good shape for visiting Grandmother and could only occasionally make the trip.

During Christmas week, my mother and I went to San Antonio. While we were there, Dad called to tell us that Bitsy had passed away in her sleep. The loss of such a beloved friend is powerful. Our grief over losing Bitsy was deep and heartfelt, but especially so for my mother and father. Yet we were comforted by an experience that followed Bitsy's passing.

Heidi's Bitsy

The morning my father found Bitsy, he buried her behind the house before leaving for work. Then he called my Aunt Sharon and told her that Bitsy had died. About fifteen minutes later, she called him back sounding rather bewildered. She asked if he had said anything to Grandmother about Bitsy's passing, and he said he hadn't.

Then Aunt Sharon told my father a strange story. She said that when she called my grandmother that morning, her first words were, "Sherry, where is Bitsy? She was here, then she left and I can't find her." My aunt was surprised, but she didn't mention Bitsy's death to Grandmother in that conversation.

Later that night, when my father got home from work, he found a message Grandmother had left on his answering machine that morning. It said, "Preston, Bitsy is with me right now. Is everything okay with her?"

That evening, my father went to the nursing home and asked Grandmother why she had left that message. She told him that, sometime during the night, Bitsy had come into her room and jumped into bed with her. Bitsy had slept at the foot of the bed, where Grandmother could see and feel her presence. Because she was too weak, Grandmother couldn't reach down and touch Bitsy. Meanwhile, in the physical realm, Bitsy had been five miles away from the nursing home and not well enough to jump up on a bed by herself.

Apparently, as in life, Bitsy wanted to pay one last visit to her Memaw. It was a testament to all of us that not only do we get to see our human loved ones when we pass over, but we also get to be with our beloved animal companions.

While we all grieved over the loss of Bitsy, I think her final farewell to Grandmother helped soften the blow.

A Heavenly Vision

Fleur Wiorkowski
Fort Worth, Texas

To me, the concept of granting souls to human beings while denying them to animals has always seemed bizarre. This belief was reinforced for me shortly after Rat Rae, one of my first rats, died. The only downside I can see to caring for rats is their short life span. Two years is considered a very long life for a rat. Rat Rae had been sick from the day I adopted her, so her life lasted only a year and six days.

I'm a vegan. I catch bugs in my house and take them outside. I truly hate having animals euthanized. Despite the fact that Rat Rae was having grand mal seizures every thirty minutes or so, the day I had her euthanized I worried about whether I had done the right thing for her.

The Sunday after Rat Rae died, I was treated to probably the most intense spiritual experience I have ever had, and it was during church service. I was taking Communion when I had a vision of Rat Rae playing with a white rat on the shoulders of Our Lord Jesus Christ. Inwardly, I was told that the white rat and his brother would be my next pair and that they were already waiting for me, curled up in a ball in the front right corner of the snake-food cage at our local pet store. It was communicated to me that I had to get this white rat the next day, Monday, or it would be too late. Most significant was the white rat's name, Noah — an ancient Hebrew word for "comforter."

On Monday morning, I went to the store and found Noah waiting for me right where I had been told he would be: in the front right corner of the snake-food cage. When I opened the cage to catch Noah, a black rat jumped out of the cage onto my shoulder. I figured this must be the second rat I was supposed to adopt, so I took them both home.

Fleur's Noah

Now both Noah and Asa have gone back to be with God. I'm sure they've joined all the other animals I have cared for, and it is only a matter of time before I see them again.

Love with Her Dying Breath

Dr. Rebecca L. G. Verna, MS, DVM, CAC, CVA, CVCH, CCRP
Marshall, Virginia

As a holistic veterinarian, I was invited by a good friend to do a house-call euthanasia. My friend is a massage therapist for humans, and she is also studying cranial-sacral techniques.

When I arrived at my friend's place, I had the odd feeling that I'd forgotten a few items. I always pack a kit for this kind of house call. For some reason, I arrived without my tourniquet, cotton balls, alcohol, or clippers. I hadn't even brought my stethoscope! Wondering what was wrong with me, I decided to let God guide me through this experience.

My friend's sister welcomed me into their home and showed me to the backyard, where the cancer patient — a cat named Miss Pippin — was lying on my friend's lap, looking restful and at peace. The two of them sat under a tree in the yard among the wildflowers.

I confessed that I had some concern about being there without the necessary equipment to prepare the cat's vein. When I finished saying this, Miss Pippin placed her foreleg in my hand and exposed her vein to me. She was letting me know that this was her choice, too. I prayed for guidance, then I clamped down the vein high on her leg to allow it to stand out and be visible. With my other hand, I slid the needle gently into her vein. It was the perfect stick. Miss Pippin purred while I slowly injected the solution.

I talked quietly to Miss Pippin and my friend the whole time. As the cat went quietly to sleep on my friend's lap, I saw a bright mental image of Miss Pippin leaping into the air to catch a butterfly in the meadow beyond the yard. My friend confirmed that Miss Pippin had always been a great butterfly chaser.

Then my friend took my hands and guided me to place them over the back of the cat's head and on her sacrum. "The cranial-sacral pulses get very strong at the time of passing," she said. "See if you can feel them."

I tried to feel the gentle, wavelike rhythm she described, and soon I was surprised to feel a soft ebbing and flowing under my fingertips, like the ocean tides. I have training in the Japanese energy-healing technique of Reiki, so I knew how to feel the cat's energy. It grew hotter and hotter under my hands during Miss Pippin's transition to the other worlds. My friend and I held the cat for a long time, until both sensations passed.

Later, we each wrote to our teachers in cranial-sacral therapy and Reiki and asked them why these energies had surged so strongly at the time of Miss Pippin's death. They both explained that the cat was trying to soothe our pain at releasing her by sending energy back to comfort us.

God bless all the little creatures and the love they share with us during their lives — and even at their deaths.

Telephone Calls and Touches

Linda Woodley

Williamsport, Pennsylvania

*M*y long-haired tortoiseshell cat, Tootie, followed me everywhere and slept by my side every night. She always needed to be touching me. Her displays of affection were truly wonderful. For example, whenever she walked by me, she'd stop and plant a kiss on my bare foot.

Tootie got cancer and died in my arms at 5:00 one evening, leaving me devastated. I stayed home from work the next day, looking at pictures of her and crying all day. About 5:00 PM that day, the telephone rang. I went into the bedroom to answer it, leaving my other cat, Felicia, asleep on the couch. I picked up the receiver and said, "Hello," but no one answered. I lay back down on the bed, and the tears flowed again. Then I felt a cold nose put a kiss on my toe, just as Tootie used to do.

Linda's Tootie

I could feel the wetness evaporate into the air. Thinking the kiss must have come from Felicia, I shook my foot to make her go away. I was still too caught up in grief to pay attention to her.

When Felicia didn't jump onto my bed, I sat up to see where she went. She was nowhere in sight. I walked back into the living room. I felt goose bumps on my arms when I saw that Felicia was still asleep, right where I'd left her when I went to answer the phone. At that moment, I realized that my angel cat, Tootie, had come back to comfort me and tell me that she was okay.

A Beautiful Light Leaves the World

Lisa Aurora Kyle
London, England

The short life of our tabby cat, Wuzzy Fuzzy, was magical. People and animals seemed to flock to him. Wuzzy Fuzzy was the apple of my eye. The most embarrassing moment in my life was when my boyfriend overheard me pledge my undying love to Wuzzy Fuzzy, vowing that if I were a cat I'd be his girlfriend.

When he was two years old, Wuzzy Fuzzy was hit by a car and killed instantly. Too upset to deal with the situation that evening, we put his body in a cardboard box. In my dream that night, I vividly saw the box standing open. The feeling that Wuzzy Fuzzy was alive was so strong that I woke up thinking it had all been a mistake and he had only been unconscious. I rushed downstairs to check the box. It was closed, and his body was still inside.

I sadly climbed back up the stairs and drifted off to sleep again. This time, in my dreams I was climbing a ladder. Balanced on my shoulders, warm and purring with his tail wrapped around my neck, perched Wuzzy Fuzzy. Up and up we climbed. Finally we reached a place where he started to sing a joyous greeting. Suddenly we were surrounded by hundreds of cats of all shapes and sizes. Wuzzy Fuzzy jumped from my shoulders and joined the group. They moved off in a pack. I saw him going away, his little tail upright as if he were off on an adventure. Then he stopped and turned to face me. I could see his tabby markings and a patch of black fur where the car had hit him. We said a loving farewell. I knew he was happy and alive on another level of life.

The next morning, as I recounted these dreams to my family and we prepared to take Wuzzy Fuzzy's body to the vet, suddenly all the electricity in the house went out; the lights, kettle, and central heating stopped. Not even our car would start. I felt this was confirmation that a beautiful light had left this world. But in my heart Wuzzy Fuzzy lives on.

Lisa's Wuzzy Fuzzy

Answers

Sherri-Lynn White
Frederickton, New Brunswick

For the longest time, I had been having inner torment about whether or not our beloved pets enter the Kingdom of God, or heaven, upon their deaths. I had heard many people say that animals have no souls, and that they cannot inherit the Kingdom of God.

Well, my precious little ferret, Jade-Elaine, has taught me a different point of view. Jade Elaine never allows his toys to be away from his goody bin, which is behind the cedar chest in my living room. Jade-Elaine keeps close tabs on that bin and checks his inventory at every turn. Even if I play with his toys to entice him to get them out, he only grabs the ones he wants and then stashes the rest right back in the goody bin.

One day, I saw Jade-Elaine sauntering down the hall with a toy in his mouth. Into my bedroom he went. "Strange," I thought. "What has gotten into him? He never takes his toys elsewhere." I thought I'd better do a little investigating.

When I went into the bedroom, I discovered that Jade-Elaine had left his little teddy bear on my side of the bed. This teddy bear wears a T-shirt that says, "Best friends are forever."

I honestly believe that, because I was wondering if animals go to heaven, Our Heavenly Father showed Jade-Elaine a way to answer my question.

The hundreds of letters we've received on after-death communication with animals show a wide variety of experiences.

People report:

- seeing shadows of the animal;
- having plants or flowers bloom at the grave site or on special anniversaries or birthdays;
- feeling the distinctive touch of the animal;
- seeing and/or feeling a spirit presence or a translucent form of the animal;
- physical signs appearing, such as food in the animal's tray or favorite toys showing up in odd places;
- seeing paw prints;
- feeling a strong sense of peace at the moment of death, as if the animal is content; and
- dreams of the animal coming back to say good-bye.

People have confided to us that they cried more when a pet died than when they lost human family members. Those who have lived with special animals understand the deep grief of losing these pure vehicles for God's love. We suggest that people give themselves the gift of grieving in their own way and for whatever amount of time it takes, and to get professional grief counseling to help them through the loss.

On a happier note, we receive hundreds of letters reporting that animals have found the most incredible ways of coming back to the people they love.

CHAPTER TWELVE

Reuniting with Loved Ones

We, as a society, have much to gain from research into the mysteries of the mind, the soul, the continuation of life after death, and the influence of our past-life experiences on our present behavior. Obviously, the ramifications are limitless, particularly in the fields of medicine, psychiatry, theology, and philosophy.

— Brian L. Weiss, MD

*L*ove lives on. When grieving people call or write to us about the loss of their animal best friends, we reassure them that the love transcends death. But these words are not mere sentimentalities. As you'll discover by reading the stories in this chapter, we reunite with loved ones in a variety of spiritual ways that are sometimes beyond what most of us might think possible.

Over the years, we've talked with people who don't believe in reincarnation for themselves, but who have had extraordinary experiences with the soul of a deceased animal returning to them in another body. Often the two animals, born months or years apart, have similar markings, characteristics, and memories.

Monica Ramsten from Helsingborg, Sweden, wrote to us about

a series of spiritual experiences and insights she had while in a contemplative state. She had inwardly asked a spiritual master named Prajapati, who offers loving service to the animal kingdom on earth and in the heavens, if she could be allowed to help in ministering to animals.

Below are excerpts from Monica's story, called "My Encounter with Animals on the Other Side." Of course, this is one woman's personal spiritual journey. As with every spiritual experience in this book, it's open to interpretation and can be filtered through your own set of beliefs. You decide if it has the ring of spiritual truth.

My Encounter with Animals on the Other Side

After my cat Knarren died, I frequently visited the astral plane (the first level of heaven after the physical plane) and began helping out with the animals there. I was guided by Prajapati.

Monica's Knarren

I came to one house where pets usually came soon after they died. It was like a home, where the animals became accustomed to what they had just gone through. This was the most difficult place to visit, because some of the animals were very sad about departing from the humans they loved. Many animals were grieving over their losses. Others were feeling relieved and loved being there because there was tremendous harmony and love.

Some were confused and did not understand where they were. Others were being healed. Still others were angry, and others were tired and wanted to rest.

All their needs were being taken care of with great understanding. Prajapati told me that the animals are never released from this home until they come out of their negative feelings and learn to let go of the past.

As soon as the animals became detached from their past life, they roamed around outside by a pond in a serene area. The view of nature in this setting was so magnificent that it is hard to describe. I loved being there.

Then I saw a school where each animal attended classes at his or her own level of consciousness. There were twelve levels of classes. Between the eighth and ninth levels, there was a kind of energy shield that the animals could not see through or go past.

Prajapati took me to a few of the initial levels of classes. At the first one, the animals were being taught about animal and human physical bodies and the natural laws.

I learned that the animals move gradually through these levels as they pick up other animal bodies and return again and again to earth. Within each class they attend, the animals go deeper into the subjects they are studying. They spend many lifetimes in the animal kingdom before they are given the chance to move to the ninth level.

After going through the shield that covers the ninth level, the animals enter a very sacred and serene place. Here, they are taught about energy and spiritual laws. These levels take a long time to go through.

Monica's story reminds us of an exercise we offer to people in our workshops if they wonder about an animal reincarnating. We tell them to look at photos of the animal companions they had earlier in their lives, then compare them with photos of animals they've had later in life. When they look into the eyes of the animals in the two photos, people often see the same soul or energy. Usually it is the look of love coming from the two pets that helps the person realize that they have been reunited with an old friend from the past. Other times, the people feel that their previous animal friend has not returned yet has guided them to a hand-picked successor.

The stories in this chapter show that there are many ways in which animals we've loved return to us. These are mystical, marvelous, thought-provoking testaments to the divine love and mercy that reunites us with our sacred companions.

Kanda's Return

Jenny Drastura
Huntington, West Virginia

*K*anda was a beautiful, stylish little Lhasa apso. She was our first show dog, and she never let us down. Always showing her little heart out, Kanda exhibited an attitude of cockiness, as if to say, "Look at me. I'm the best!"

Kanda's favorite toy was a small, squeaky latex pig. In spite of the fact that she was surrounded by other toys that belonged to all four of our dogs, she played only with those pigs. None of the other dogs cared at all about them.

We began buying Kanda a new toy pig at every dog show. Her collection soon consisted of fourteen of the little treasures. She played with all of them at one time or another. If we took one away from her and hid it among the other toys, she found it immediately. She jumped up on the couch, balanced the pigs on her paws, and swatted them across the room so that she could chase them. When the pigs got caught in something, Kanda insisted that we retrieve them for her or she would get very huffy. Kanda had us well trained.

At dinnertime, when she heard the food bowls, Kanda would go crazy, playing with one of the pigs and making the strangest throaty noises. I think the sound of the food made her hungry, and in her mind she was hunting and chasing. She made those toys squeak and squeak and squeak.

Coming home from work was always a joy for us. When we opened the front door, Kanda frantically searched for just the right pig so that she could greet us at the door with her selection. We had to squeak the pig for her, or she'd be horribly insulted.

Just three weeks before her third birthday, Kanda received a routine vaccination. About five hours later, she went into convulsions. By the time we reached our veterinarian twenty minutes later, Kanda was comatose. Although she regained some of her natural functions, such as eating, her brain waves were flat-lined. She died eight days later.

Words can't express the sorrow our family felt over Kanda's death. The thought of never seeing her again was unbearably painful. Not wanting to say a final good-bye, I left all of Kanda's toy pigs in the living room where she had last played with them. As always, the other dogs ignored them.

Kanda's birthday came soon after her death. I decided to entwine the pigs I had bought at the shows into a bouquet of flowers and place them on her tombstone. While preparing the bouquet, I started to cry. I said to my husband, "We will never hear Kanda squeak those pigs again."

Immediately Suki, our somewhat lazy Lhasa who had never looked at one of the pigs in her life, got up, walked over, picked up a pig that was lying on the floor, and squeaked it for about two minutes. Then she plopped it down and walked to the other side of the room to resume her usual sleeping position.

We were stunned and speechless. It was clear that Kanda had not gone anywhere; she was still with us. But we also knew that Kanda was too active and assertive to come back for very long in the body of laid-back Suki. Besides, the two girls didn't like each other much.

We wanted another Lhasa who would be as close to Kanda as possible, so I began looking for a puppy who was related to her. I found out that Kanda's littermate had had puppies, but when I called to inquire about them it didn't work out for us to adopt one.

The next year, we decided to adopt a female Lhasa and have our own puppies. We asked the breeder of our male to select a female who would be a good match for the dog. My husband and I drove to the breeder's house to pick up the female. We brought the puppy home, but her pedigree was not yet ready, so we anxiously awaited it in the mail. Meanwhile, we named our new puppy Daisy because of the way golden hair grew like daisy petals around her little black nose.

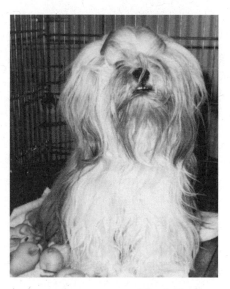

Jenny's Kanda

Daisy was only sixteen months old. According to our breeder, the little girl was fearful and shy. When we brought Daisy home, we saw that she indeed needed a lot of attention to get over her insecurities. At first, she shuddered and quivered in the corner of our kitchen and cowered when we approached her. We tried everything to soothe Daisy, but she was still afraid. Finally we took her into the living room, away from the household noises, and handed her one of Kanda's pigs.

The transformation was incredible. Daisy immediately began making the pig squeak. Then she ran to the chair, jumped up, balanced the pig on her paws, and swatted it across the room just like

Kanda used to. She played and played, ignoring us — also as Kanda always did when she was preoccupied with her toys. Daisy got the toy pig caught in the same places Kanda had, expecting us to retrieve it for her. And she even found Kanda's same hiding places for the toy.

The next day, when Daisy heard the food bowls, she grabbed a pig and began playing frantically with it, making those same strange sounds in her throat that Kanda used to make. We were overjoyed when, on the following day, we came home from work and Daisy greeted us at the door, expecting us to squeak the pig she carried in her mouth.

Within that first week, we received Daisy's pedigree. That was when we learned that Daisy is the daughter of Kanda's littermate — one of the same puppies we had tried to adopt a year earlier. Daisy had been a pick puppy, which is how our breeder came to have her, but the breeder hadn't known that we were looking for one of Kanda's nieces.

We knew Kanda was back. We concluded that Daisy was the niece Kanda had been waiting for so that she could make her appearance again. The transformation of Daisy from a fearful, shy puppy to an outgoing, cheeky brat had taken place before our eyes.

According to experts in reincarnation, the ability to recognize belongings from earlier lives is a sign that a soul has reincarnated. Perhaps the same soul that animates Daisy also animated Kanda.

For more than one thousand years, the Lhasa apso has been an important part of the religious history of Tibet, developed and nurtured by the spiritual leaders of Buddhism. Ancient literature even claims that if a Buddhist monk leads an exemplary life, he will be reincarnated as a Lhasa apso, since the dogs are so highly revered.

Because of our belief that Kanda lives on in Daisy and will be with us always, we took Daisy to receive a special blessing from a Buddhist monk.

Just like Kanda, Daisy has never let us down. She finished her championship and has given birth to beautiful puppies. At the age of ten, she still swats and bounces and squeaks those toy pigs, as only she and Kanda could do best.

Meditation

Toys, familiar places, regular habits — these are some of the ways we can figure out if an animal has reincarnated. Have any of these signs and wonders occurred with animals who may have more in common with each other than you thought?

Miss Kitty Returns Her Love through Ally McPurr

Lisa Sherman
Greensboro, North Carolina

A few years ago, my beloved Miss Kitty crossed over the Rainbow Bridge on a summer day. She was my first "baby," and the absence of her purring, snuggling with me in bed, and joining me every afternoon for "kitty cocktails" was the most heartaching experience I had ever encountered.

Miss Kitty was a beautiful silver-shaded Persian-mix with brilliant green eyes. People often told me how beautiful she was, but I felt that I was the only one who really knew how deep her beauty went. I believe that Miss Kitty sensed my feelings about her. She certainly was always there for me when I needed her.

I often referred to Miss Kitty as my "Persian princess." On the morning of Princess Diana's funeral, my family (husband Steve, Miss Kitty, and me) was watching the procession together. As the tears streamed down my face, Miss Kitty snuggled up to me and licked them away. I believe she knew how sad I was, and she comforted me at the loss of this modern-day princess.

Miss Kitty often met me at the door after a long day at work. We would share some quiet moments together until it was time to make dinner. Our favorite times were in front of the fireplace on a cold winter's night. My husband has many photographs of his two girls snoozing cozily together — usually lying so that we mirrored each another.

One afternoon shortly after Miss Kitty died, a friend was consoling me. This friend is very intuitive. She said that Miss Kitty would always be looking over us, and she sensed that Miss Kitty would send another cat to complete our family. This new cat, she predicted, would probably test me to be sure that my love for her was indeed true. She thought that whoever Miss Kitty sent would not be another beautiful, glamorous Persian princess but an everyday kitty.

Lisa's Miss Kitty

Over the following months, several friends called to tell me about cats who needed homes, but I wasn't ready to bring another puss-pal into our family. I was still grieving over my baby and needed more time.

One Sunday morning in October, I awoke feeling troubled. My husband asked if I'd had a bad dream. I told him that, for the first time since her death, I'd dreamed about Miss Kitty. In the dream, I was smelling her fur and just loving her.

After breakfast, my husband and I went outside to do some gardening chores. Overnight, we'd had our first frost. The perennials needed trimming, and the dahlias needed lifting. While we were working, a neighbor came over with a cute but unremarkable-looking brown-striped tabby. She asked if we knew where the cat had come from, but we didn't. She told us that she couldn't keep this cat because she had an outdoor male tomcat who wouldn't like sharing his domain with a newcomer.

Well, the tabby looked hungry, and I did have food that had belonged to Miss Kitty. I hadn't been able to bear throwing it away. So I put out some food, and that poor little tabby cat ate four bowls full. She was starving!

As my husband and I wandered around our garden that day, this little missy followed me everywhere. Her attentiveness to our activities was amusing. We continued our garden chores with this frisky feline charging up and down the paths, showing curiosity about everything we did.

At one point, my husband found a bag of tulip bulbs and asked where I wanted to tuck them in for the winter. I told him that I wanted to plant them at Miss Kitty's grave. As my husband planted the bulbs at Miss Kitty's grave site, this new tabby jumped up onto my shoulders. That's when I realized that Miss Kitty had indeed been looking out for us; she sent us this little tabby. My friend's prediction had come true.

That afternoon, just in case the kitten's human family was looking for her, we posted signs all over the neighborhood and at nearby shopping centers. I knew that the tabby must have had a home, because she was wearing a flea collar. The next morning, we called local vets and shelters. For days, I scanned the classified section of the newspaper, searching for anyone who had lost a tabby. But there were no calls, no answers. How could this be? A sweet little "tabby delight" like her needed a loving family and a good home.

As the days rolled by without answers to our inquiries about her family, we realized that she was here to stay and that we needed to find a suitable name for this little purr machine. After much deliberation, we named her Ally McPurr. "Ally" because she came to us as a stray and was so thin, like the Ally McBeal TV character, and "McPurr" for the constant hum of her purring.

Later I put more pieces of this puzzle together. Miss Kitty had originally lived at the house where our neighbor had found the tabby cat. We had adopted Miss Kitty from the people who lived there because she was unhappy being the only cat in a home with a Doberman and three little boys, all under the age of six. A few months later, the family moved away without saying good-bye to our Persian princess.

Lisa's Ally McPurr

Even more interesting, I'd had only one dream about Miss Kitty, and it was on the night before Ally McPurr came into our lives. Surely the fact that Ally had jumped onto my shoulders while we were planting at Miss Kitty's grave site must be more than chance.

Since that October morning, Ally McPurr has become the new joy of our lives. My husband says she is my cat when she does what we call "kitty-kooking" — racing insanely all over the house. I say she is his cat when she paws at the window blinds in the early-morning hours and awakens us. But, in truth, she is our cat. We both love her dearly.

Every year on the anniversary of Miss Kitty's passing, I put flowers on her grave and bring a bouquet home for Ally. Each October 25, we have a birthday party for Ally to mark the anniversary of her coming to us and enriching our lives far more than I ever imagined an eight-pound ball of fur could.

In my heart, I know that Miss Kitty sent Ally to be with us. Miss Kitty found a sweet little feline who needed a loving home, and she brought us all together.

Meditation

Have you had signs that an animal who has gone to the Rainbow Bridge sent just the right creature to heal your broken heart?

The White Dog Nobody Saw

Rita M. Romansky
Venetia, Pennsylvania

On October 4, 1996, our beloved German shepherd, Kheva, suffered a massive coronary and died while my husband and I were both at work. We phoned our priest, Father Pat, and he came right over and blessed Kheva. We also shared the blessing with Kheva's housemate, Tasha, a black-and-white Siberian husky.

After preparing Kheva for burial, we grieved all evening. Late that night, we were so distraught that we drove to the rectory because we couldn't console ourselves. Father Pat told us not to worry because this day was the feast of Saint Francis of Assisi, the patron saint of all living creatures. He assured us that Saint Francis was taking care of Kheva now.

The next morning, still heartbroken, we decided not to go to work but to spend quality time with Tasha, who would not leave the bed where Kheva had slept.

On the following morning I had to return to work, but my heart was still heavy with sadness. As I left our cul-de-sac and proceeded up the road to the four-way stop, I noticed a man in his driveway putting his suitcases in the trunk of a car.

Since traffic was stopped in front of me, I had to stop. While I casually observed the man, a large, solid white dog ran in front of him and headed toward the road. I got out of my car and called to the dog, a beautiful white German shepherd. The dog stood in front of me, wagging his tail and smiling.

Almost startling me, two men — the man with the suitcases and a man who'd been in the car behind mine — approached and asked me what was wrong. Why was I standing in the road in the morning darkness talking to thin air?

I asked the men if they had seen the white German shepherd. Both were bewildered by my question. They looked at each other and told me there had been no white dog. I was stunned. Surely at least one of them would have noticed such a beautiful, unusual-looking animal, but they hadn't!

Rita's Kheva

I got back into my car and thought about what had just happened. The only explanation I could come up with was that although Kheva was tan and black in his physical body, he had come back as a white dog in spirit to tell me that he was okay and happy. I wondered if Saint Francis had something to do with Kheva's appearance to me.

When we received Kheva's ashes, I bought a Saint Francis medal and asked Father Pat to bless it. I carefully placed the medal in Kheva's urn along with his favorite ball. Somewhere, sometime I will be reunited with my beloved Kheva. God bless this happy soul.

Meditation

Have you considered asking Saint Francis to help you know if your dear animal companion is only gone physically, but still with you spiritually?

Come Back Soon

Diana Stewart-Koster
Wishart, Queensland, Australia

*W*hen I was a young mother, I spent a few months' holiday with my parents in Sierra Leone, West Africa, where my father worked as a civil engineer. While living there, my parents had acquired an African gray parrot they named Poll Parrot. She took a strong dislike to my mother and seemed to be jealous of her. Poll was generally friendly, but whenever Mum attempted to offer her a snack, the bird would try to bite her. If Dad gave Poll the same morsel, she would take it immediately. But Mum loved Poll Parrot and liked to sit beside her on the veranda. The bird's cage was half-protected from the elements by the veranda roof and half-exposed so that Poll could bathe and sun herself. Every day when Mum had her morning or afternoon tea, she would chat with Poll as though talking to a friend.

Soon Poll Parrot was speaking very clearly in my mother's voice. Poll Parrot would call the household staff, who would come running to the veranda only to find that the bird had beckoned them. Poll Parrot would also call the dogs and mimic many phrases she'd overheard. She would say, "Good morning, Parrot. Morning, bird," in my father's voice. She never said "good morning" at night; she knew the times of day and the movements in the house.

When my parents left West Africa, Poll Parrot came to stay with me in South Africa for a few years. I grew to love the bird. At other times, some of my sisters took her. Eventually, my parents retired and settled in South Africa, at which time Poll Parrot went back to them.

As a family, we had grown up on the move. So it was no surprise that, within a decade or so, one of my sisters and I immigrated to Australia. One day we received a phone call from Dad, saying that Mum was ill and dying. We hurriedly left for South Africa, and were fortunate to spend some time with Mum while she was still conscious and could understand that we were there to help Dad and be with them both. Mum died within a week of our arrival, and I stayed on for a month to help Dad.

Poll Parrot continued to remind us of Mum's presence as she called each of my sisters in Mum's voice. She had remembered our names within a couple of days of our arrival.

Diana's Poll Parrot

On the day of my departure, I was filled with sadness. It was five o'clock in the morning as I left the house. I went to Parrot and said, "Good-bye, Parrot." Clearly and distinctly, as though my mother was standing beside us, Poll Parrot replied in Mum's voice, "Come back soon."

Since I believe in reincarnation, I wondered if this farewell from Poll Parrot might actually be a prediction. Perhaps this was God's way of telling me that the soul that had been my mother was going to return to my life soon.

Now we come to the present, and I have a granddaughter. When she was three years old, I asked her if she remembered when she was big — in other words, if she could recall another lifetime. Her instant reply was, "I remember when you were little and you drank my milk," and she cradled an imaginary babe to her chest. I have no doubt that my mother *has* "come back soon" — as my granddaughter. I can spend time with her in a different way, continuing to share the love that we built up for each other over many lifetimes.

Today I have my own African gray, whom I named Poll Parrot. I smile every time he says "Come back soon" when I leave the house. But Poll Parrot has added another phrase to his large repertoire. He also calls out, "Bless this day."

And God does.

As the end of our journey together nears, we extend our hand in friendship to all of you who have loved and been loved by an animal. We, Allen and Linda, and this book's coeditors — Leaf, Cuddles, Speedy, and Sunshine — are immensely grateful that you've chosen to spend time with us and the wonderful people who have shared their inspiring experiences.

"Angel animals" not only bless your life on earth but also help you from the other side. We are grateful for the continued spiritual presence of Prana, Feisty, Sparkle, and Taylor. To those of you who have been parted from a beloved animal companion, we offer condolences for your loss and hope for the future. As the stories in this book show, death can only separate you physically. The souls who loved you in life are never far away, even after death.

If you're like the thousands of people we have been honored to meet, animals are serving to uplift you spiritually. Sometimes before we speak at a book event, we say to the bookstore manager, "Watch the people who come in the door. Animal lovers are the most compassionate and generous people on the planet." We speak about you with confidence because we know that when you relate to animals in a loving and respectful way, you have the opportunity to learn from some of life's wisest teachers and to be restored by its most skillful healers.

Animals open a pathway for God to communicate with and support you. They prove that you are never alone or abandoned. Animals deliver unconditional love and mercy from the Divine, even if your heart has been hardened by suffering or broken by disappointment.

Animals watch your movements constantly. Their eyes dart to and fro, silently observing as you scurry about your daily life. We hope that after reading this book and reflecting on its messages, you'll be inclined to turn the tables and start paying closer attention to the animals in your life.

Albert Schweitzer once wrote, "Reverence for life comprises the whole ethic of love in its deepest and highest sense."[1] We encourage you to even go beyond reverence. Allow yourself to be edified and enlightened by the bright sparks of God in animal bodies. They live as your spiritual partners on this earth. Through their actions and their love, they can teach about the Divine better than all the wise words in the world.

Notes

Introduction: Golden Connections

1. Kristin von Kreisler, *Beauty in the Beasts: True Stories of Animals Who Choose to Do Good* (New York: Tarcher, 2001), 15–16.

2. Shankar Vedantam, "Baboons Demonstrate Ability to Learn Complex Mental Task," *Washington Post*, 15 October 2001, A02; Tim Friend, "Culture's Not Only Human: Powerful Evidence Suggests That Animals Pass On Learning," *USA Today*, Tuesday, 5 June 2001, 6D; Sharon Begley, "Aping Language: New Studies Suggest That the Brains of Chimps Possess the Same Structures for Syntax and Meaning That Ours Do," *Newsweek*, 19 January 1998, 56–58.

3. Laura Tangley, "Animal Emotions: Sheer Joy. Romantic Love. The Pain of Mourning. Scientists Say Pets and Wild Creatures Have Feelings, Too." *U.S. News & World Report*, 30 October 2000, 48–52.

4. Michael Fox, "Pets Can Respond to Affection by Revealing Their Intelligence," *St. Louis Post-Dispatch*, Infonautics, 1997.

Chapter Four:
Angel Animals Heal Hurting Hearts, Bodies, and Minds

1. Dr. Marty Becker with Danielle Morton, *The Healing Power of Pets:*

Harnessing the Amazing Ability of Pets to Make and Keep People Happy and Healthy (New York: Hyperion, 2002), 19.

Chapter Five:
Are Prayers Answered?

1. Andrew Newberg, MD, Eugene D'Aquili, MD, and Vince Rause, *Why God Won't Go Away: Brain Science and the Biology of Belief* (New York: Ballantine, 2001), 15.
2. Sharon Begley, "Religion and the Brain: In the New Field of 'Neurothology,' Scientists Seek the Biological Basis of Spirituality. Is God All in Our Heads?" *Newsweek,* 7 May 2001, 50–57.

Chapter Six:
Why Do Bad Things Happen?

1. Harold S. Kushner, *When Bad Things Happen to Good People,* twentieth-anniversary edition (New York: Schocken, 2001).
2. The Holy Bible, the New King James Version, published by the American Bible Society (New York: Thomas Nelson, 1983), 804.

Chapter Seven:
Are We Mirrors for Each Other?

1. Ranny Green, "We Lavish Love, Money on Our Pets: Study Reveals Psyches of Animal Owners," *Seattle Times* and *St. Louis Post-Dispatch,* 12 July 1993.
2. Deepak Chopra, *The Return of Merlin* (New York: Harmony, 1995).

Chapter Nine:
Do Animals Help Us Have Strength to Survive Troubled Times?

1. Kahlil Gibran, *The Prophet* (New York: Knopf, 1941), 25.

Chapter Ten:
Do Dreams of Animals Contain Spiritual Messages?

1. George Howe Colt, "The Power of Dreams," *Life* (September 1995): 36–49.
2. Melissa Kaplan and William K. Hayes, *Iguanas for Dummies* (Hoboken, NJ: Wiley, 2000).

Chapter Eleven:
Do Animals Go Peacefully into the Light?

1. Dwight Ott, "Will Your Pet Rise Again? Yes, Some Faiths Say," *Philadelphia Inquirer*, 7 February 1999.
2. Kathleen Laufenberg, "Special Report: Animals Destined for Death," *Tallahassee Democrat*, posted 4 August 2002 on www.Tallahassee.com.

Chapter Twelve:
Reuniting with Loved Ones

1. Albert Schweitzer, *Reverence for Life*, translated by Reginald H. Fuller (New York: Harper & Row, 1969), 117.

Permissions Acknowledgments

Part One: Love

Meister Eckhart (1260–1327), quoted in *Animal Blessings: Prayers and Poems Celebrating Our Pets,* compiled by June Cotner (San Francisco: Harper-Collins, 2000), 133.

Chapter One:
How Do Animals Remind Us of the Divine?

Rachel Naomi Remen, MD, introduction from *My Grandfather's Blessings: Stories of Strength, Refuge, and Belonging* (New York: Riverhead, 2000), 2–3. Used by permission of Riverhead Books, an imprint of Penguin Group (USA) Inc.

Chapter Two: Hearing the Whispers of Love

The Holy Bible, the New King James Version, published by the American Bible Society (New York: Thomas Nelson, 1983), 600.

Chapter Three: Choosing to Be Together

The Bhagavad Gita, translated by V. Sadanand (Madras, India: Sadanand, 1977), 490.

Chapter Four:
Angel Animals Heal Hurting Hearts, Bodies, and Minds

Antoine de Saint-Exupéry (1900–1944), quoted in *A Guide for Grown-Ups: Essential Wisdom from the Collected Works of Antoine de Saint-Exupéry,* compiled by Jennifer Ward (San Diego, CA: Harcourt, 2002), 71.

Portions of "Ferrets Are Made of God" by Rebecca Stout were previously published in *Modern Ferret* magazine.

Part Two: Wisdom

Kabir, *The Bijak,* Number 182, translated by Bob Hayes, © 2002.

Chapter Five: Are Prayers Answered?

Excerpted from *Children's Letters to God* © 1991 by Stuart Hample and Eric Marshall. Used by permission of Workman Publishing Co., Inc., New York. All rights reserved.

The poem "Walk Easy" by Sandy Carlson was first published in *laJoie: The Journal That Honors All Beings.*

Chapter Six: Why Do Bad Things Happen?

Gaelic folk saying, quoted in *A World Treasury of Folk Wisdom,* compiled by Reynold Feldman and Cynthia Voelke (New York: HarperCollins, 1992), 66.

Chapter Seven: Are We Mirrors for Each Other?

Japanese Zen saying, quoted in *A Zen Harvest: Japanese Folk Zen Sayings* compiled and translated by Sōika Shigematsu (Berkeley, CA: North Point Press, 1988), 32.

"Forest Family" by Harold Klemp from *Stories to Help You See God in Your Life,* ECK Parables, Book 4, by Harold Klemp, pp. 161–62, copyright © 1994 by Eckankar. Reprinted by permission of Eckankar, P.O. Box 2000, Chanhassen, MN 55317-2000, www.eckankar.org. All rights reserved.

Part Three: Courage

William Blake, "The Tyger," *The Complete Poetry and Prose of William Blake,* revised edition, David V. Erdman, ed. (Berkeley and Los Angeles: University of California Press, 1982), 24.

Chapter Eight: Angel Animal Heroes

Korean folk saying, quoted in *A World Treasury of Folk Wisdom* (New York: HarperCollins, 1992), 91.

Chapter Nine: Do Animals Help Us Have Strength to Survive Troubled Times?

Homer, *The Iliad,* translated by Richmond Lattimore (Chicago: University of Chicago Press, 21st impression, 1971), 8:135, 186.

Part Four: Comfort

Thich Nhat Hanh, *Living Buddha, Living Christ* (New York: Riverhead, 1995), 53. Used by permission of Riverhead Books, an imprint of Penguin Group (USA) Inc.

Chapter Ten: Do Dreams of Animals Contain Spiritual Messages?

John Boyle O'Reilly, "The Cry of a Dreamer," *The Best Loved Poems of the American People,* Hazel Felleman, ed. (New York: Doubleday, 1936), 145–46.

Chapter Eleven: Do Animals Go Peacefully into the Light?

The Best Loved Poems of the American People, Hazel Felleman, ed. (New York: Doubleday, 1936), 314.

Chapter Twelve: Reuniting with Loved Ones

Brian L. Weiss, MD, *Many Lives, Many Masters* (New York: Fireside, 1998), 5. Copyright © 1998 by Brian L. Weiss, MD. Used by permission of Simon & Schuster Adult Publishing Group.

Contributors

Chapter One: How Do Animals Remind Us of the Divine?

MARY ELIZABETH MARTUCCI, "The Dog Who Discovered God." Mary Elizabeth has shared her home with precious animals since childhood. Whether dog, cat, rabbit, bird, turtle, or lamb, each provided loving, memorable lessons.

MARY ELLEN "ANGEL SCRIBE," "Q: Is There a God? A: Meow!" Mary Ellen is a "Pet Tips 'n' Tales" newspaper columnist, internationally known author of *Expect Miracles* and *A Christmas Filled with Miracles* (Conari Press, 2000), and an award-winning photojournalist. Her famous swimming cats can be seen on www.AngelScribe.com. You can contact Mary Ellen at AngelScribe@msn.com.

ROSE-MARIE SILKENS, "The Presence of Teddy." At the time Rose-Marie wrote her story, she was a writer and gardener on northern Vancouver Island, where she also operated a small plant nursery. Her beloved friend Teddy died three years after the experience in her story occurred.

MONICA O'KANE, "Send in the Cows." Monica is a wife, mother of eight, grandmother of sixteen, and great-grandmother of one. She is the author of *Hey, Mom, I'm Home Again! Strategies for Parents & Grown Children Who Live Together* (Marlor Press, 1992). She is a child-rearing activist who focuses on childbirth and breastfeeding. In 2001 Monica traveled to Romania to work in a soup kitchen for two weeks because the homeless children there had caught her interest.

AUBREY FORBES, "Season's Eternal Song." Aubrey has read original poetry to large audiences across North America and facilitated workshops on creating spiritual poetry. He has several works in progress. His email address is aaforbes@qwest.net.

Chapter Two: Hearing the Whispers of Love

LYNN HARPER, "The Man Who Didn't Like Cats." Lynn is San Diego's number one female talk show host (www.lynnharper.com). She loves her husband, Bill, and they both love Sage (Ms. Americat), Hugo (mini-schnauzer), mini-Bill (they both have silver beards), Mitzvah and Kyng Mydas (turtles), and assorted tropical fish.

RON MIROLLA, "A Triple Play of Unconditional Love." Ron is a nutritionist who works with the terminally ill and people with eating disorders. His work is taxing, but his dog was always there to comfort him and those with whom he worked. He does dog rescue work with the Rescue Train in Los Angeles and Aussie Rescue of Southern California. His Aussie rescue work is inspired by his current dog, who has partially filled the hole created in his heart when Triple left this earth.

SAMUEL DUFU, "God's Love and the Snake." Samuel is the chairman of the ARB Apex Bank, the Mini Central Bank of all the Rural Banks in Ghana. He is married and has four children. He enjoys researching spiritual matters.

J. BLAIR TAYLOR, "The Journey of Joy." J. Blair is a freelance writer, photographer, and animal appreciator. She lives with her husband, three children, two dogs, one cat, two rabbits, three squirrels, and (depending on the season) as many as eleven wild rabbits.

MEG MACZURA-BETTS, "Max's Miracle of Love." Meg is a dental assistant who is forever thankful to God and her husband for Max, their loyal companion of eighteen years. He is a blessing.

KATHIA HAUG THALMAN, "A Coyote's Message." Kathia is a professional language translator from Pazzallo, Switzerland. She welcomes emails at khaug@bluewin.ch.

Chapter Three: Choosing to Be Together

DONNA FRANCIS, "Abbie Knew Best." Donna is involved in deaf-education and animal-assisted therapy. She shares her home with five dogs and three cats. Abbie passed away in 2008.

ANABELA GUERREIRO, "All in the Family." Anabela lives in Mississauga, Ontario, Canada, and shares her life with her husband, Manuel, and their Brazilian cat, Niko.

DORIS ROUSE, "That Special Someone." Doris is an active fund-raiser for her local humane society. She has seven cats and eight dogs. Her cat Buffy is no longer alive.

ELLEN MOSHENBERG, "Matchmaker, Matchmaker, Make Me a Match." Born in Connecticut, Ellen now lives in Arad, Israel, where she is a medical librarian in Beer Sheva, Israel, and an English correspondence assistant to a renowned novelist and peace activist. She is married and has two children in college, one dog, and about twenty cats. All her pets are rescues. Ellen is the international representative for the Cat Welfare Society of Israel, a member of the local Arad L'chai Animal Organization, and a member of the Israeli peace movement and Meretz civil rights party.

R. DALE HYLTON, "Cindy Finds Our Friends." For thirty-four years, R. Dale was an investigator, consultant, and advisor for the Humane Society of the United States. He developed the Humane Society's youth program and was editor of the monthly *KIND News Magazine*.

LISA ALTIERI-O'BRIEN, "Mr. Kitties, the Grief Counselor." Lisa and her loving husband, Eric, share their home with their two sons, Nathaniel and Gabriel, their cat, Bootsie Kitty, and their dog, PeeWee. Sadly, Mr. Kitties passed away at the age of sixteen on October 30, 2006, due to complications from diabetes. You may contact Lisa at la9691@aol.com.

Chapter Four:

Angel Animals Heal Hurting Hearts, Bodies, and Minds

REBECCA STOUT, "Ferrets Are Made of God." Rebecca can be reached at wolfysluv@aol.com.

JUDY TATELBAUM, "The Compassion of Noodles." Judy Tatelbaum, MSW, is a grief therapist and the author of *The Courage to Grieve* (HarperCollins, 1984) and *You Don't Have to Suffer* (HarperCollins, 1989). Noodles lived well to age fourteen. Now Judy works with her dog Honey. You may contact Judy at www.judytatelbaum.com or 800-4COURAGE.

RUBY M. HANNA, "A Hamster's Legacy." The pets in Ruby's life include everything from farm animals to doves and hamsters. She is a retired teacher and a cofacilitator of a creative project, "A Write to Joy."

MARY MARGARET MCEACHERN, "Kitten Launches a Law Career." Mary Margaret is an attorney with her husband, Robert E. Dillow, Jr., in Dillow, McEachern & Associates, P.A., in Wilmington, North Carolina (www.dillow andmceachern.com). Kitten passed away from cancer. Their pets currently are Buddy Fuzz and Eight Ball.

LINDA L. NICKERSON, "Bon Jour Helped Mary Have a Good Day." Linda uses positive reinforcement to train American miniature horses for visits to nursing homes and special-education classes. Her website is www.geocities .com/hastylinda/minis.html.

Part Two: Wisdom

KABIR, *The Bijak*, Number 182, translated by Bob Hayes, © 2002. Bob is a translator, an educator, and codirector of a spa and an institute dedicated to healing and expressive arts. He lives on a ranch in Veracruz, Mexico.

Chapter Five: Are Prayers Answered?

SIERRA GOODMAN, "Amazing Grace and the Dolphin." Sierra is president of the Vida Marina Foundation of Costa Rica, a nonprofit foundation working to create a marine sanctuary off the coast of Drake Bay, Costa Rica, to protect more than twenty-five species of dolphins and whales inhabiting the area. Visit www.vidamarina.org for more information.

PAULA TIMPSON, "A Meditating Angel Dog." Paula is a poetess who lives in Stonybrook, Long Island, with her husband, Jimmy, and their spirited son, Jamesey. Paula writes about nature and God daily in her poetry. Her website is http://paulaspoems.blogspot.com.

THE REV. MARY PIPER, "A Moose Messenger." The Rev. Mary Piper and family share their lives with seven dogs (six are rescues), three rescue cats, five horses, and a variable number of other rescue animals. She's an Episcopal priest and a hospice chaplain.

CATHERINE KIRK CHASE, "The Miraculous Opening of a Heart." Catherine, her husband, Lawrence, and son, Jacob, share a happy life with their dogs, Grace and Kayla; their kitties, Bob, Betty, Angel, and Rami; and Finnegan, the clown fish.

SANDY CARLSON, "Walk Easy." Sandy joyfully shares her home in Woodbury, Connecticut, with her daughter, Adella May. The dog who inspired "Walk Easy" now runs with the hounds of heaven.

Chapter Six: Why Do Bad Things Happen?

RICHARD SIMMONS, "Spotted Angels." For over thirty years, Richard Simmons has had the unique ability to deliver a serious message through laughter to millions of Americans via videos, Deal-A-Meal and FoodMover programs, personal appearances, television appearances, infomercials, cruises, and his website, www.richardsimmons.com. He is the author of nine books, including three bestselling cookbooks, *Richard Simmons' Never-Say-Diet Book* (Grand Central Publishing, 1982), and *Still Hungry after All These Years* (GT Publishing Corporation, 1999). In 2004 he launched "Hoot Camp" in Los Angeles to teach fitness teachers and coaches how to motivate their students to overcome childhood obesity.

KAREN LEE STEVENS, "Cassidy and Our Date with Destiny." Karen is an animal advocate and the author of *All for Animals: Tips and Inspiration for Living a More Compassionate Life* (Fithian Press, 2001). She is founder of All for Animals, Inc., a pro-animal educational organization dedicated to raising awareness about cruelty-free living and the importance of compassion for all animals. For more information, visit www.allforanimals.com.

LYDIA CHIAPPINI, "A Llama with Wings." Lydia is an art professor, fiber artist, illustrator, and the author of *The Llama Who Wished for Wings* (Lydia Chiappini, 1998). She is the llama lady of Heaven's Gate Llama Farm. She has also written and published *Claude's Wings and Vincent's Toes* (1999), *Picotee the Polka Dotted Llama* (2000), *For Love of Claude* (1999), and *A Llama's Tale* (2003). She is working on a new book, *The Llama Who Went to College.*

LORRAINE LANZON, "The Upside-Down Birdhouse." Lorraine is a retired registered nurse. Her family consists of two daughters, one son, and several grandchildren. She and her twin sister were raised with singing yellow-gold canaries.

LOIS STANFIELD, "Explaining to a Horse How It's All in Divine Order." Lois is a photographer, a digital artist, and an avid horsewoman. You can contact her at lois@lightsource-images.com or www.lightsource-images.com.

Chapter Seven: Are We Mirrors for Each Other?

EVELYN ALEMANNI, "Sacred Companions." Evelyn is a freelance technical writer, artist, and garden enthusiast. She lives in Elfin Forest, California, and shares her home with her husband, Joe, and three basset hounds. Her website is www.allea.com.

GRACE J. HARSTAD, "Seeing Parallels, Finding Omens." Grace is a retired physical therapist and certified Feldenkrais practitioner who lives in Brentwood, California. She can be reached at gharstad@aol.com.

JANETTE WARREN, "The Falcon's Return." Janette is a CranioSacral and Lymphatic Drainage therapist and is a teaching assistant for the Upledger Institute. Her passion is "unwinding" long-held tissue trauma, especially of the brain and nervous system. Humans and animals benefit from her nutritional products, which support the heart, the brain, the immune, digestive, and nervous systems, and detoxification. She is a servant and a lover of all of life. For more information, visit www.iahp.com/janettewarren or email janette.warren@gmail.com.

LARRY SIEGEL, "Simple Gifts." Larry is a composer/performer and can be seen with his animal and human family at www.larrysiegel.com. His music fills people with joy and an unshakable feeling that this is a wonderful life.

HAROLD KLEMP, "Forest Family." Sri Harold Klemp is the spiritual leader of Eckankar, a religion that teaches that animals, just like people, are souls, too. Sri Harold writes extensively and has produced more than forty published works to date, including *Animals Are Soul Too!* (Eckankar, 2005). This story is from his book *Stories to Help You See God in Your Life,* ECK Parables, Book 4. For more information, visit www.eckankar.org. Reprinted with permission of Eckankar. All rights reserved.

Chapter Eight: Angel Animal Heroes

PATRICIA A. BROWN, "A Dog's Life." Gonzo has passed on, but his memory and love live on forever in Patricia's heart. "Thank you, my friend," she says.

DAVID YOUNG, "The Dog Who Knew His Place." David is a veteran of the U.S. Army and is a surgical assistant studying to be a physician's assistant. He is married to Cherie.

LAUREN L. MERRYFIELD, "Kabootle, Our Rescue Cat." Lauren lives in Washington with her cats, Gabrielle, Maryah, and Lewie. Her husband, Jim, died in 2007. Lauren is a member of the Cat Writers' Association, the Association for Pet Loss and Bereavement, and the National Federation of the Blind. She edits *CATLINES*, an online newsletter (www.catliness.com). You can contact Lauren at 877-816-9887 or lauren1@catliness.com.

ILONA SELKE, "Warnings from the Dolphins." Ilona is the author of *Wisdom of the Dolphins* and *Dolphins, Love & Destiny* (Living from Vision, 2008). She teaches worldwide with her husband, Don Paris, PhD, about the cocreative power of the mind and how to access the mystery of the soul. Their powerful manifestation course *Living from Vision* is available online at www.lfv course.com or by calling 800-758-7836.

DOROTHY WEISS, "Divine Spirit Sends in the Birds." Dorothy is the author of a memoir, *Alice's Lantern*. She and her husband, Monroe, a musician, enjoy the harmony, diversity, and beauty they observe in nature's creatures.

Chapter Nine: Do Animals Help Us Have Strength to Survive Troubled Times?

DIANNE ARMSTRONG, "The Dog Who Loved TV." Dianne is a registered nurse. She shares her home with her husband, Ron; her miniature schnauzers, Rainy and Mattie; and her shelties, Dillon and Patrick. Dianne and Ron run Montana Pets on the Net (http://montanapets.org).

DONNA MOODY, "Our Angel Kitty." Donna believes that animals are good therapy because they give unconditional love. Loving dogs and cats is a big part of her life.

CAMILLE A. LUFKIN, "The Luck Bunny." Camille lives in the Adirondack Mountains with her "StealthBunnies" and several other "stealth critters." Visitors are welcome at the Lair of the StealthBunnies (http://members.tripod .com/stealthbunny). Camille's blog is at http://stealthbunny.livejournal.com.

NANCY HARLETT, "Support through a Team Effort." Nancy is a solo folksinger and entertainer, widely known as "Patchwork Nancy." As a folk legend, Nancy appeals to young and old alike with her music and jokes. Her singing group is Eagle River with Patchwork Nancy. A music historian, Nancy researches the backgrounds of the songs she sings, some of which date back hundreds of years, and shares the history with her audiences. She lives with ten cats in Tiffin, Ohio, in a house that was built in 1810. Listen to Patchwork Nancy's folksongs at www.folkalley.com/openmic/artist.php?id=1010. You can email Nancy at nharlett@yahoo.com.

ALLEN AND LINDA ANDERSON, "A Squirrel Reminded Us to Trust God."

Chapter Ten: Do Dreams of Animals Contain Spiritual Messages?

SHARON WARD, "I Dreamed of DeeDee." Sharon lives in Raleigh, North Carolina, with her husband, Ron, and their five cats, Bandi, Chiva, Deedee II, Elmo, and Fubbi. Visit their website at www.ronwardphotography.com.

HOPE CATHERINE BALL, MED, "Dreaming of My Animal Spirit." Hope is working in psychiatric research in Florida. She lives with her animal friends Leopold, Satchmo, Wolfgang, and Cinder.

DARRY CONNER, "An Iguana's Nightmare." Darry and Ted Conner were owned by Bubbette for eight wonderful years before God decided that Bubbette had earned her angel wings. She will always live in their hearts. Darry is a cofounder of TriangleIguanaRescue.com in North Carolina. To learn more about Bubbette, visit www.geocities.com/conne009mcdukeedu.

RICHARD S. MCDIARMID, "The Doggie Dream Diagnosis." Rick is a professional artist and workshop facilitator. He and his wife, Dianne, live in British Columbia, Canada, with their dog, Misha, and cat, Purdy. Visit his website at www.richardsmcdiarmid.com.

LESLIE-ANN GUINEY, "The Cat Who Guided My Dad Home." Leslie-Ann shares her home with two cats, Connie and Alistair, and a yellow Lab, Brody. She works for the Centre for Addiction and Mental Health as the manager in administration for the Education & Publishing Unit. She spends her spare time with her partner, James, and studying for her degree in criminal psychology.

LAURENCE CRUZ, "White Horse Dream." Laurence is a freelance writer in Los Angeles. You may reach him at cruzcoms@earthlink.net.

Chapter Eleven: Do Animals Go Peacefully into the Light?

JUDY NEELY, "Messengers from Heaven." Judy shares her home with the spirit of her Boston terrier Molly; six Boston terriers — Megan Mcq, Promise, McKinsey, Quincy, Elliott, and Brooklyn; several Arabian horses; and two cats. She is a nurse and also works with Boston Terrier Rescue. Judy may be reached at ladysmcq@aol.com. You can see pictures of Molly at www.dreamscape.com/mishwahr/molly2.htm and at the Boston Terrier Memorial website (www.dreamscape.com/mishwahr/memorial.htm).

HEIDI W. DUNLAP, "Bitsy Says Good-Bye." Heidi is an artist, massage therapist, and Reiki Master. She and her husband, Jerry, share their home with their shelter-found cat, Cassie.

FLEUR WIORKOWSKI, "A Heavenly Vision." Fleur currently cares for several rat and cat companions, all of whom get along quite well. You may contact her at fwiorkowski@hotmail.com.

DR. REBECCA L. G. VERNA, MS, DVM, CAC, CVA, CVCH, CCRP, "Love with Her Dying Breath." Dr. Verna is certified in animal chiropractic and veterinary Chinese herbology. She is a certified veterinary acupuncturist and certified canine rehabilitative practitioner. She is a Reiki Master and also practices using applied kinesiology, Chinese and Western herbology, flower essences, and homeopathics.

LINDA WOODLEY, "Telephone Calls and Touches." Linda collects cats and angels. She shares her home with her two cats, Kalli and Kasey. Linda's email address is angelkatz@chilitech.net.

LISA AURORA KYLE, "A Beautiful Light Leaves the World." Lisa left music production to pursue a path of healing and self-mastery. She shares her discoveries through workshops and is a Reiki Energy Master and animal communicator.

SHERRI-LYNN WHITE, "Answers." Sherri-Lynn's "Fab Four" are together again at the Rainbow Bridge. She misses Jade-Elaine, Daisy Mai Amber-Lynn, and Nikki Taur. She plans to have more ferrets in the future.

Chapter Twelve: Reuniting with Loved Ones

MONICA RAMSTEN, "My Encounter with Animals on the Other Side." Monica is a therapist and shares her home with six cats.

JENNY DRASTURA, "Kanda's Return." Jenny is a university magazine editor and freelance writer. She has been involved in showing Lhasa apsos and Maltese for twenty-three years. She and her husband are owned by twelve dogs, five of whom are rescues.

LISA SHERMAN, "Miss Kitty Returns Her Love through Ally McPurr." Lisa shares her home with Ally McPurr and her husband, Steve. She also runs her own landscaping business.

RITA M. ROMANSKY, "The White Dog Nobody Saw." Dr. Michael and Rita Romansky have always enjoyed having German shepherds. Kheva was their first. They are blessed with three today: Makoa, Bekka, and Keela.

DIANA STEWART-KOSTER, "Come Back Soon." While Poll Parrot was alive, she headed Diana's family of children, grandchildren, dogs, cats, alpacas, cockatiels, cows, and hens, and was the best of all.

Acknowledgments

We give our appreciation to Georgia Hughes, New World Library's editorial director, who has worked with us on *Angel Animals Book of Inspiration* to bring the book's messages to the world.

We are grateful to the wonderful visionary Marc Allen, the marketing director and associate publisher Munro Magruder, our enthusiastic publicity manager Monique Muhlenkamp, managing editor Kristen Cashman, type designer Tona Pearce Myers, art director Mary Ann Casler, proofreader Karen Stough, eagle-eyed editorial assistant Jonathan Wichmann, and all the staff at New World Library.

We sincerely appreciate the encouragement from Harold and Joan Klemp, which inspired us on our journey of giving service by writing books about the animal-human spiritual bond.

A special thanks to all the people who shared their stories about the many cherished experiences with pets and animals in nature.

We extend our heartfelt gratitude to Stephanie Rostan of Levine Greenberg Literary Agency, Inc., our dynamic literary agent, whose middle name is Encouragement.

Our families instilled a love of animals in us from an early age. We especially appreciate Allen's mother, Bobbie Anderson, and Linda's mother, Gertrude Jackson. To our son and daughter, Mun Anderson and Susan

Anderson: you're the best. Much love to Allen's sister, Gale Fipps, and brother, Richard Anderson, and their families.

Special thanks to Darby Davis, editor of *Awareness* magazine, for publishing our column, "Pet Corner," all these years and to Kathy DeSantis and Sally Rosenthal for writing consistently beautiful book reviews. To Lessandra MacHamer: you have always been in our corner, and we love you for it.

And thanks to our current animal editors, Leaf, Speedy, Cuddles, and Sunshine. Without you, we wouldn't have been able to fulfill our purpose.

About Allen and Linda Anderson

*A*llen and Linda Anderson are speakers, pet-expert consultants, and authors of a series of books about the spiritual relationships between people and animals. Their mission is to help people discover and benefit from the miraculous powers of animals. In 1996 they cofounded the Angel Animals Network.

In 2004 Allen and Linda Anderson were recipients of a Certificate of Commendation from Governor Tim Pawlenty in recognition of their contributions as authors in the state of Minnesota.

In 2007 their book *Rescued: Saving Animals from Disaster* won the American Society of Journalists and Authors Outstanding Book award.

Allen Anderson is a writer and photographer. He was profiled in Jackie Waldman's book *The Courage to Give*. Linda Anderson is an award-winning playwright as well as a screenwriter and fiction writer. She is the author of *Thirty-Five Golden Keys to Who You Are & Why You're Here*. Allen and Linda teach writing at the Loft Literary Center in Minneapolis, where Linda was awarded the Anderson Residency for Outstanding Loft Teachers.

The Andersons share their home with a dog, two cats, and a cockatiel. They donate a portion of revenue from their projects to animal shelters and animal-welfare organizations.

You are welcome to visit Allen and Linda's website at www.angelanimals.net

and their home pages and groups on Facebook (search "Linda-Allen Anderson"), MySpace (www.myspace.com/angelanimals), and Beliefnet (Angel Pets Fan Club, http://community.beliefnet.com/?page_id=1107&group_id=661). Send them stories and letters about your experiences with animals. At the website or by email, you may also request a subscription to their free email newsletter, *Angel Animals Story of the Week*, which features an inspiring story each week.

Contact Allen and Linda Anderson at:
Angel Animals Network
PO Box 26354
Minneapolis, MN 55426
Website: www.angelanimals.net
Email: angelanimals@angelanimals.net